Physical Characteristics of the Pekingese
(from the American Kennel Club breed standard)

W9-CLB-127

Proportion: Length of the body, from the front of the breast bone in a straight line to the buttocks, is slightly greater than the height at the withers. Overall balance is of utmost importance.

Body: Pear-shaped and compact. It is heavy in front with well-sprung ribs slung between the forelegs. The broad chest, with little or no protruding breast bone, tapers to lighter loins with a distinct waist. The topline is level.

Tail: Base is set high; the remainder is carried well over the center of the back. Long, profuse straight feathering may fall to either side.

Hindquarters: Lighter in bone than the forequarters. There is moderate angulation and definition of stifle and hock. When viewed from behind, the rear legs are reasonably close and parallel and the feet point straight ahead.

Coat: Body Coat: Full-bodied, with long, coarse textured, straight, stand-off coat and thick, softer undercoat. The coat forms a noticeable mane on the neck and shoulder area. Feathering: Long feathering is found on the back of the thighs and forelegs, and on the ears, tail and toes.

Color: All coat colors and markings, including parti-colors, are allowable and of equal merit.

Size/Substance: Stocky, muscular body. All weights are correct within the limit of 14 pounds, provided that type and points are not sacrificed.

Pekingese

◇

By Juliette Cunliffe

Contents

KENNEL CLUB BOOKS: PEKINGESE
ISBN: 1-59378-253-5

Copyright © 2000 • **Revised American Edition: Copyright © 2003**
Kennel Club Books, Inc., 308 Main Street, Allenhurst, NJ 07711 USA
Cover Design Patented: US 6,435,559 B2 • Printed in South Korea

Photographs by Carol Ann Johnson, with additional photographs by:
Norvia Behling, T. J. Calhoun, Carolina Biological Supply, Doskocil, Isabelle Français, James Hayden-Yoav, James R. Hayden, RBP, Bill Jonas, Dwight R. Kuhn, Dr. Dennis Kunkel, Mikki Pet Products, Phototake, Jean Claude Revy, Alice Roche, Dr. Andrew Spielman and C. James Webb.

Illustrations by Renée Low.

The publisher would like to thank the owners of the dogs featured in the book, including Maria Castro, Anthony & Elizabeth Deck, Gloria Henes, Edith N. Jones, Roxanne Luchesi, Miss Winnie Mee, Lorraine Moran, Nicolas Odette, Sylvia Roznick, Alice & Robert Sohl, Ev Spaulding, Susan Speranza and Elizabeth Tilley.

Eng. Ch. Chu-Erh of Alderbourne, owned by Mrs. C. Ashton
Cross and painted by Lilian Cheviot in 1907.

HISTORY OF THE

PEKINGESE

The Pekingese boasts an enormously rich history and is deservedly a breed that enjoys great popularity throughout the world. Bred meticulously by sovereigns of Imperial China for centuries, the Pekingese was a special favorite in the royal palaces, where he was kept separately from the other castle dogs.

Those kept in the palaces were of finer quality than the Pekingese kept by the commoners, the latter being somewhat larger and coarser in general appearance. Dogs of the royal households were occasionally presented to other Eastern monarchs and doubtless some of their bloodlines filtered through to other breeds of the East. The Japanese Chin, Pug, Tibetan Spaniel and the charming Happa Dog, meaning "under-the-table" dog, who looked rather like a short-coated Peke, are some obvious examples. Although breeds such as these are still distantly related, their relationship in the Middle Ages was much closer than it is today.

It is believed that in early times, the Pekingese was owned only by the highest court dignitaries, those of royal blood. Just as commoners were forbidden to look at the Emperor, so were they obliged to turn away their heads, upon pain of death, whenever the Pekingese appeared. Certainly this little dog was held in the greatest esteem; some say it was almost sacred. There were even Pekingese that had high literary awards bestowed upon them. One was given the official Order of the Hat, which might be compared to today's Nobel Peace Prize!

THE PEKINGESE IN ART
From Chinese art, we can see clearly that the Pekingese and the Pug were two quite separate breeds; this was evident in the Imperial Chinese brushwork. Thousands of years before the Christian era, dogs appeared on Chinese bronzes, and later there were small lion-like dogs found on pottery and porcelain. In Chinese Buddhist art, a sacred mythological lion was much used in symbolic form and eventually the Pekingese dog itself was allowed to represent this symbol.

Paintings from the 17th and 18th centuries give us a fairly

clear insight into dogs bred in the Imperial Palace, for court artists were often commissioned to paint dogs housed in the Palace. There was one particular scroll of note, tenderly portraying 100 dogs, painted by Tsou Yi-Kwei.

In art of the 18th century, the Pekingese generally conformed to a rather conventional pattern. The dog was always uniform in its markings and always had a similar expression, with large goggle-eyes. Even as late as the end of the 19th century, the Dowager Empress Tzu Hsi, famed for her love of the Pekingese, followed this style in her own paintings, as did her painting instructress.

The famous Pekingese breeder, Mrs. Vlasto, and two of her famous champions: See Mee of Remenham, born in 1922, on the left and Remenham Dimple, born in 1923, on the right.

Indeed there are many valuable works of Chinese art, rich in their portrayal of the "Lion Dog," as the Pekingese was called. Many of these are housed in museums open to the public, but there are many others in private collections. During the 19th century, the paintings more closely resembled living dogs, and these could be found as beautifully painted miniatures, on fans, snuff bottles, lanterns, screens and caskets.

THE EMPRESS TZU HSI

As a Princess in Peking, Tzu Hsi was inordinately fond of all small animals and singing birds, always finding time to attend to her animal friends. In later life, she was affectionately known as "Old Buddha" and she continued her interest in breeding dogs to the end of her days as Empress.

Before Tzu Hsi's time, small dogs customarily had their growth stunted with mechanical devices and drugs. This enabled them to be carried in ladies' sleeves in court, giving rise to the name "Sleeve Dog." The Empress, however, restricted these methods and encouraged natural methods, including selective breeding as a means of keeping size down.

The majority of her Pekingese was sable or rich red in color, but she liked many colors and certainly also had black, parti-colored and white ones. It was even said that some of her dogs were bred to match the color of the peonies and the fruit that grew along the shores of the lakes on the grounds of the Summer Palace.

Although the quotation is lengthy, no book about the Pekingese would be complete, in the author's opinion, without including an interpretation of Empress Tzu Hsi's description of and advice about the Pekingese. These words were delicately described as "pearls dropped from the lips of Her Imperial Majesty Tzu Hsi, Dowager Empress of the Flowery Land of Confucius:"

Let the Lion Dog be small;
Let it wear the swelling cape of
    dignity around its neck;

Let it display the billowing stan-
    dard of pomp above its back;

Let its face be black;
Let its forefront be shaggy;
Let its forehead be
    straight and low,
Like unto the brow of an Imperial
    harmony boxer.

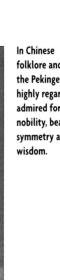

In Chinese folklore and art, the Pekingese is highly regarded, admired for his nobility, beauty, symmetry and wisdom.

Let its eyes be large and luminous;
Let its ears be set like the sails of
     a war junk;
Let its nose be like that
     of the Monkey God of the
     Hindus.
Let its forelegs be bent,
So that it shall not desire to
     wander far,
Or leave the Imperial Precincts.

Let its body be shaped
Like that of a hunting lion spying
     for its prey.
Let its feet be tufted
With plentiful hair that its footfall
     may be soundless;
And for its standard of pomp,
Let it rival the whisk of the
     Tibetan yak,
Which is flourished to protect the
     Imperial litter
From the attacks of flying insects.

Let it be lively,
That it may afford
     entertainment by its gambols;

Let it be discreet,
That it may not involve itself in
     danger;
Let it be friendly in its
     habits,
That it may live in amity with
     other beasts,
Fishes or birds that find protec-
     tion in the Imperial Palace.

And for its color
Let it be that of a lion—a golden
     sable,
To be carried in the sleeve of a
     yellow robe,
Or the color of a red bear,
Or of a black bear, or a white
     bear, or striped like a dragon
So that there may be dogs
Appropriate to each of the Imper-
     ial robes.

Let it venerate its ancestors,
And deposit offerings in the dog
     cemetery
Of the Forbidden City on each
     New moon.
Let it comport itself with dignity
Let it learn to bite the foreign
     devils instantly.

Let it be dainty in its food
That it shall be known as an
     Imperial dog
By its fastidiousness.

Sharks' fins
And curlews' livers
And the breasts of quails, on these
     may it be fed;
And for drink

EARLY COLORS

Most Pekingese bred during the breed's first 60 years in the West were red with dark masks, but there were also fawns, blacks, black-and-tans and a few whites, though these often turned cream in adulthood. The first pure white strain was established in the 1920s. Liver color with chocolate points was also known.

*Give it the tea that is brewed from
    the spring buds
Of the shrub that grows in the
    province of Hankow,
Or the milk of the antelopes
That pasture in the Imperial
    Parks.
Thus shall it preserve its integrity
    and self-respect
And for the day of sickness let it
    be anointed
With the clarified fat of the leg of
    a sacred leopard,
And give it to drink a throstle's
    eggshell full of the juice
Of a custard apple in which has
    been dissolved three pinches
Of shredded rhinoceros horn, and
    apply to it piebald leeches
So shall it remain–but if it die,
Remember, that thou too art
    mortal!*

The Empress was extremely conscientious and methodical, both in her work and in her play, and though at times she could be flexible, at others she could be quite ruthless. She undoubtedly became one of the greatest Empresses of the East and was compared in her way to Queen Victoria. The Dowager Empress Tzu Hsi died in November 1908. The following year, her remains were buried, with a funeral costing half as much as any previous royal funeral. A favorite Pekingese was carried to precede the Imperial bier to the tombs. This was Moon-tan, meaning "peony," who had a yellow and white spot on the forehead. The event was reminiscent of the death of Emperor T'ai Tsung some 900 years earlier. His dog, Tao Hua, meaning "peach flower," followed his master to his last resting place, and there died of grief, it is said, at the portal of the Imperial tomb.

It was said that the Empress's dog also died of grief, but others believe Moon-tan was smuggled away and sold by one of the eunuchs.

Sun Chi of Greystones with His Highness Pratap Singh, Maharajah of Nabha in the 1930s.

THE ARROW WAR

A war, known as the Arrow War, was waged between China and the Western Allies in the 1860s. The Imperial household was evacuated from Peking shortly before the invaders arrived in the Forbidden City. However, five Pekingese dogs were left behind at the Summer Palace. These were believed to have belonged to an aunt of the Emperor, who had chosen not to flee, but instead to stay behind and commit suicide. British officers seized these dogs and took them to Britain, these being the first known Pekingese to have arrived on these shores. One of these five was exceptionally small and was carried around in the forage cap of Lt. Dunne. She was renamed "Looty" and was presented to Queen Victoria, in whose care she remained until her death in 1872.

Looty was fawn and white in color and weighed but 3 lb. She was not heavily feathered and rather more resembled a Lo-sze, which was a kind of smooth-haired Pekingese. It seems likely that Looty lived at Windsor Castle, but she probably spent most of her days in the kennels there, rather than as one of the pets in the castle. A painting of her was made in 1863, this by a pupil of the renowned artist Sir Edwin Landseer.

The other four Pekingese were brought to Britain by Lord John Hay and Sir George Fitzroy. The

Eng. Ch. Ko Tzu of Burderop, born in 1910, bred and owned by Mrs. E. Calley, won 20 Challenge Certificates before World War I temporarily ended dog showing in Europe.

two brought by the former were a black and white dog, Schlorf, and a bitch, Hytien, who weighed a little over 4.5 lb and was a rich chestnut color with a dark mask. Lord Hay gave these to his sister, the Duchess of Wellington, and with the aid of the dog, who lived to the ripe old age of 18, she was able to keep the breed going at Strathfieldsaye. The other two were both fairly small, dark chestnut in color, with dark masks. It was from these two that the famous Goodwood strain was produced.

There are various accounts of the ransacking of the Summer Palace, which took place in the latter part of 1860. One account tells readers that six Pekingese were thrown down a well, instead of being left for the "foreign devils." Indeed, wells were used for many things besides water, including disposal of the Emperor's chief concubine! It is highly likely that more dogs were smuggled outside the Palace, and that these were sold by the eunuchs to high-ranking Chinese nobles. Certainly a few dogs were later found beyond the palace walls, and these were thought to closely resemble the exquisite dogs of the Palace.

ESTABLISHMENT IN BRITAIN

As we have seen, breeding of the Pekingese took place at Strathfieldsaye and at Goodwood, and

The famous British show dog, Eng. Ch. Tai Yang of Newnham, bred and owned by Mr. Herbert Cowell, won 40 Challenge Certificates in the 1930s. This was a record for any breed during those times.

by the late 1890s there were at least 17 Pekes at Fulmar Palace in Slough, with Lord John Hay. He called these dogs Peking Spaniels and wrote most interesting accounts of their antics. They even sailed across the lake on little rafts and performed wonderful gymnastic feats!

The Goodwood Kennels were already famous, for they had been built in 1787 to house the Goodwood Pack of Foxhounds. By the late 19th century, it seems likely that the Pekingese were kept as pets in Goodwood House, where other small breeds had been looked after. Goodwood's Duchess of Richmond gave some Pekingese to intimate friends. At this time, appropriately enough, many of the breed's main supporters were members of the aristocracy.

From the end of the Arrow War, through the Boxer Rebellion of 1900 and until the death of the Empress Tzu Hsi in 1908, many westerners had connections with China. Consequently, dogs of genuine Pekingese type, and some less so, were brought to Britain during this time. Most of these early importers were army officers.

Going back to 1860, when the five Pekingese dogs were found in the Summer Palace, there were reports that another 14 "odd-looking little dogs" were found upon bursting open a locked door. Two of these dogs came to England in 1863. Lara and Zin, the latter a pure white Pekingese, were presented as a wedding gift to Lord and Lady Hay. Zin suffered an accident and was replaced by another dog, named Foo. It is probable that the first two of these were Chinese-bred.

It is all too easy to become bogged down in the fascinating

PEKINGESE CLUB
In 1898, it was the Japanese Spaniel Club that drafted a breed standard for the Pekingese, but in 1900 the club's name was changed to Japanese and Asiatic Spaniel Association. From this developed the Pekingese Club, in 1902, followed soon after by the Peking Palace Dog Association.

events of those early decades of the breed's history in the West. In 1885, a brace was sent to Britain from China by Admiral Sir William Dowell. There also was a dog given by a Palace eunuch in exchange for medical services rendered. This dog is counted among several influential early

Madam of Winwood and Little Joke of Winwood represent the breed in the 1930s.

stud dogs of repute and commanded stud fees of five or ten guineas, a considerable sum in those days.

The breed was becoming highly popular and strengthening in numbers. England's national breed club was formed in 1904, and of course the Pekingese was assisted by some influential breeders. Mrs. Clarice Ashton Cross started her highly influential Alderbourne Kennel after World War I, and there were many breeders of merit between World Wars I and II.

THE PEKINGESE ARRIVES IN THE US

It was not until after the Boxer Rebellion that the Pekingese appeared in the USA. The Dowager Empress Tzu Hsi made gifts of dogs to several influential American society women; among them was Theodore Roosevelt's daughter, Alice, who was given a black dog.

Occasional specimens were smuggled out of Peking, but this was hazardous, and eunuchs caught involved in such acts were liable to suffer death by torture. The first of the breed to be shown in the US was a dog called "Pekin;" this was in 1901. However, Americans interested in breeding Pekingese tended to look toward Britain for their imports.

According to the American Kennel Club (AKC), it first registered the Pekingese in 1906. Just a couple of years prior, T'sang of Downshire had appeared in the show ring at Cedarhurst, Long Island. He was owned by

Queen Alexandra with one of her favorite Pekingese, from a famed painting by Sir Luke Fildes, on display at the UK's National Portrait Gallery in London.

Eng. Ch. Tien Joss of Greystones, photographed in 1915, was a valuable sire during that period.

Mrs.Morris Mandy, who had come from Britain to live in the United States. T'sang of Downshire was the first of the breed to complete his championship, and, in 1908, the first Pekingese bitch to gain a Champion of Record title was Chaou-Ching-Ur, bred by the Dowager Empress and owned by Dr. Mary Cotton. It was sad that Chaou-Ching-Ur, who was black, left no offspring, but it is believed that the first official British and American breed standards were based on her.

Mrs. F. M. Weaver, in 1912, with her famous Sutherland Ouen Teu Teng, was credited with keeping the breed true to the old type.

From the time that the Pekingese became officially recognized in America, it grew in popularity, with fanciers getting together to help advance the breed. This resulted in the formation of the Pekingese Club of America (PCA) in 1909, with Mrs. Mandy and Dr. Cotton as two of its founding members. Mrs. Mandy became the club's first acting president. The club's main sponsor was Mr. J. P. Morgan, who also served as honorary president and was an extremely well-known fancier of the breed in its early years in the US.

The breed standard of England's Pekingese Club had been drawn up some five years prior to the American standard, and the PCA decided to adopt the first version of its own standard from the former. In this way, the parent clubs of Britain and the United States similarly outlined ideal breed characteristics, initially implementing a weight limit of 18 lb (8.2 kg). This was out of line with the average weight of original Chinese imports to both countries, these having weighed between 3 and 9 lb (1.4-4.1 kg). Later, the American club altered the weight clause and made any weight over 14 lb (6.4 kg) a disqualification. This indeed has been the only disqualification in the AKC standard, and remains so up to the present day.

Today, there are many AKC-licensed Pekingese clubs across the vast expanse of the US, so it is sadly impossible to pay tribute to all of them individually. Clubs bring enthusiasts together, to work for the betterment of the breed. In America, there are Pekingese clubs doing an enormous amount of good work, particularly for rescued Pekes, which is highly commendable.

Founded in the northeastern US, the Pekingese Club of America is one of the oldest clubs in the country and held an independent winter specialty show in New York City as far back as 1911. This was an inaugural event held in the fashionable ballroom of the Plaza Hotel, and attracting 94 dogs. Indeed the club has a stunning history and has historically presented a large selection of solid silver trophies to its winners. Most distinguished of these trophies is the Lasca McLuyre Halley perpetual trophy, the largest ever offered at a dog show. This, and the J.P. Morgan Trophy, can be seen on permanent

Eng. Ch. Meng of Alderbourne, bred by Mr. B. Boxley in 1928, was exported to India, where it was used in the development of the breed in that country.

An ancestral asset was Ta Fo of Greystones, bred by Miss Heuston in 1910.

display in the Library of the American Kennel Club in New York. Just once a year they are removed from their display case for presentation and cherished photographs with the Best of Breed and Best Opposite Sex winners at the PCA's winter specialty. This is now held in conjunction with the Empire Specialties Associated Clubs Inc., just prior to the Westminster Kennel Club show.

The club's summer specialty show began in 1917, but in the early years many of the big wins were dominated by British imports. This led, in 1936, to the imposition of a restriction to

The Pekingese was recognized by the American Kennel Club in 1906. Some of the first of the breed to arrive in the US were from the Empress Tzu Hsi herself, while others were imported from Britain.

"American-Breds Only" for the winter specialty, while the summer show remained open to all. Now both specialties are open to all, with these major events attracting entries from all over the world.

Until 1991, all specialty shows were held in the Northeast, but since then there has been a Rotating National Specialty weekend, held in a different of six regions of the country each year. This incredible weekend is the largest Pekingese breed event of the year, with two or even three breed shows held back-to-back, and sometimes combined with an all-breed show. The Rotating National Specialty weekend is an important date on the calendars of Pekingese enthusiasts, for there is also a Judge's and Breeder Education seminar, hosted by the Pekingese Club of America, a dinner, and auction and other merriment of repute.

One of the PCA's many publications that will be of special interest and help to Pekingese breeders is a booklet written by Thomas K. Graves, DVM, DACVIM. This is entitled *Common Medical Disorders of the Pekingese*, and proceeds from its sale benefit the Pekingese Charitable Foundation, Pekingese rescue and education.

Pekingese enthusiasts in America today must undoubtedly be grateful for the enormous amount of hard work that has been put into the club by those dedicated to the breed, some of whom have served in their offices for many a long year. Indeed, Mrs. Michael Van Buren perhaps set the ball rolling by being its President for 40 years, starting in 1913! Now the Board of Directors of the Club has representatives from every region of the country.

Revered as the original lion dog, the Pekingese has become a worldwide favorite breed due to its size, personality and intelligence.

PEKINGESE

Apart from the breed's attractive good looks, the Pekingese is an absolutely charming little dog, possessing dignity and quality, combined with a fearless, loyal temperament. Known familiarly as "Pekes," many people adore them, even if they don't own one, and it is easy to understand why the breed is so well-loved.

Its coat is appealing, but to keep the coat of Pekingese in good condition takes a considerable amount of work, so it is essential to bear this carefully in mind before deciding that this is the breed for you.

PHYSICAL CHARACTERISTICS

This is a small, sturdy dog, one that should look small but be surprisingly heavy when picked up. Ideal weight is not more than 14 lb, and no mention is made of size differences in males and females. Unlike those of most other breeds, though, Pekingese males are often a little smaller than the fairer sex. No height specifications are set forth for the Peke.

The Pekingese is thick-set, with a large head, proportionately wider than deep. The

DEALING WITH OBESITY
Elderly Pekes, like other breeds, can be prone to putting on excess weight. The profuse coat deceives an owner into thinking that the dog is of correct weight, when in fact he is overweight. Overeating or feeding the wrong foods may be the cause. Often an older dog requires a slightly different diet than a younger dog.

Pekingese are found in many colors. All colors are permissible and equally prized from a show point of view.

round, dark eyes are lustrous, and with the Peke's short nose and black pigment, it is difficult not to fall in love with this very special breed.

COLORS AND COAT

A full coat on a Pekingese is the breed's crowning glory, but to keep a coat in this condition certainly involves time and dedication. Not only does the Peke have a long coat but it also possesses a thick undercoat, not to mention a large mane covering the shoulders and long whiskers that grow down from the bottom jaw. This means that merely grooming the top layer of the coat may initially give a reasonably good overall appearance, but, in no time at all, the undercoat will start to form knots.

Knots and tangles are incredibly difficult to remove if allowed to build up, so this aspect of coat care must be taken seriously into consideration before setting one's heart on the breed.

Short daily grooming sessions can be great fun for both owner and dog, and brushing should start from the time your new puppy arrives in your home. The Peke does shed some hair regularly, and brushing has the added benefit of keeping the hair loss under control. Good coat management will benefit not only the appearance of your dog but also his health. An unkempt coat can become the breeding ground for parasites and, because of the density of the coat, this can go unnoticed until the health of your dog has been

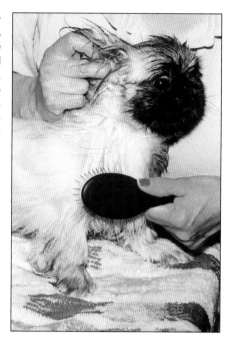

As with all long-haired breeds, Pekes require daily brushing and periodic bathing. With regard to coat, this is considered a high-maintenance breed.

Because there is no color preference in Pekingese, in truth an owner should not be swayed by color. Having said that, it is only natural that some people have a purely personal preference, just as they might for the color of their clothing or furniture. What really matters is the quality of construction of the dog, the dog's temperament and the coat quality. However, if choosing a pet, color may indeed be a deciding factor, and this is entirely understandable. After all, there is no point to buying a black Peke and then thinking for the next 14 years or so that it is a pity you didn't have the golden color you really preferred!

affected. The nose wrinkle needs daily cleaning; owners must make this part of the everyday routine.

The Pekingese can be found in a wide variety of colors, for all are permissible and of equal merit. Parti-colored dogs should have their colors evenly broken up. By looking at just a few of the pictures in this book, you will see something of the splendid array of colors in which the breed can be found. Although there is actually no mention of a black mask in the breed standard, most breeders and judges do like Pekes to have one, toning in beautifully with the lovely black nose.

TAILS
The tail of the Pekingese is set high and carried tightly, slightly curved over the back, so it is unlikely to do as much damage around the home as might the enthusiastic wagging of the tail of a large dog such as a Dalmatian or Labrador Retriever. However, the long feathering on the tail will need regular attention and grooming, so must never be neglected.

DEWCLAWS
Although there is no stipulation as to whether or not dewclaws should be removed on the Pekingese, many breeders do like to have them removed when

puppies are three days old. This makes the nails easier to manage under the long adult coat.

If your Pekingese has not had his dewclaws removed, they must be checked and clipped regularly. Dewclaws will not wear down naturally, for they do not come into contact with the ground. If allowed to grow too long, the nails will grow around and become embedded in the legs, causing great pain and probably requiring veterinary attention.

PERSONALITY

Although a Pekingese should be fearless, it is not an aggressive breed. However, a Pekingese should not be timid. Indeed, the breed has long been known for its rather majestic disregard of other creatures, a feature that fascinated the Empress Tzu Hsi.

Dignified though he may be, many a Peke thoroughly enjoys playing with a toy, though owners should consider that, because of the breed's short foreface, Pekes need fairly flat

Once you fall in love with the Peke, it's hard to stop at just one! Caring for a group of Pekes is a full-time grooming task.

Pekes are rightly called lap dogs, given their size, ornamental appearance and temperament.

toys. They are not able to grip round toys, such as balls. In general this is not a destructive breed and a suitable toy will usually quite satisfy a Peke's demand for something on which to chew.

Many people seem to be of the opinion that Pekes do not really require exercise, but that is not strictly true. Dogs of all kinds need exercise to maintain good body tone and to prevent obesity. Pekes, however, are quite happy to simply stroll around the backyard if that is what suits an owner's lifestyle. Of course, most are also perfectly happy to go for a walk, but brambles should be avoided because of the coat. It should also be remembered that Pekes can move very quickly when they choose to do so!

SLEEVE PEKES

Pekingese known as "Sleeve" Pekes are miniature versions of the breed, weighing less than 6 lb. They can be produced within a litter of normal-sized puppies, even when both sire and dam are of the usual size. Some breeders like to retain good "sleeve" males for use at stud, but such tiny bitches are rarely used for breeding, as they might well produce normal-sized puppies and would therefore have a difficult time giving birth.

Sleeve dogs were always highly prized by China's Imperial family, and they still have many dedicated followers today. They even have their own special Sleeve Dog Club. Usually a Peke puppy that will end up as a "sleeve" can be picked out early on, probably looking quite "grown-up" at an early age.

HEALTH CONSIDERATIONS

Despite being a small dog, and one with a short foreface, the Pekingese is generally a healthy, hardy breed. It is said that the Pekingese seems to have an inborn resistance to disease and that many have remarkable powers of recovery. It is difficult to ascertain why this might be so, but it could date back to the careful selective breeding in China's Imperial Courts.

When feeling ill, a Peke, like many other dogs, can be rather cantankerous, but it is to his credit that he will certainly make every effort to recover quickly. Although not every illness can be covered in a book of this nature, clearly to be forewarned is to be forearmed, so the following may be useful to give prospective owners an idea of some of the problems that might, just possibly, arise. These potential issues should be considered right along with the breed's other characteristics to help you decide if the Peke is the right dog for you.

NOSE AND THROAT

The Pekingese is a brachycephalic breed, meaning that the nasal bones are short, indicated by the breed's shortened foreface. Because of this, the Peke is more likely to suffer from nasal and respiratory problems than longer faced breeds, although, thanks to careful breeding, these problems occur much less frequently than they used to. However, any excessive wheezing or sniffling should certainly be checked by a vet,

A lovely Peke showing a desirable black mask, contributing to the breed's very distinct and special expression.

LEGEND HAS IT
According to legend, a lion met a marmoset in a forest and the two fell in love. Because of their size difference, the lion approached Buddha, praying to be made smaller. This was agreed, the lion sacrificing size and strength, but keeping his large heart, form and dignity. Our beloved Pekingese resulted from this unlikely union.

even if only for reassurance that there is nothing wrong.

A common abnormality in all brachycephalic breeds, and one of the most common problems seen in the Pekingese, is stenotic nares (pinched nostrils). This is a congenital problem in which the nasal cartilage is not formed correctly and thus can cause breathing difficulty. It is inherited, although not much is known about its mode of inheritance. Although present at birth, the problem may not become evident until later in the dog's life. Owners should be aware of the symptoms, which include noisy or strained breathing, unwillingness or inability to exercise, fainting or the dog's turning blue. Of course, veterinary attention is necessary, and there are both medical and surgical treatments for stenotic nares. Other problems that cause breathing problems in brachycephalic breeds include elongated soft palate and malformation of tissues, which can block the dog's flow of air.

Some Pekes are susceptible to sore throats and tonsillitis, but these, though uncomfortable, are not usually very serious and can be quickly treated. Sometimes, however, they can be a prelude to some other illness so must be investigated. Pekes can also sometimes suffer from what is much like a human cold, with sniffling and a slight fever. Again, when detected early, veterinary attention can usually remedy this without too much trouble.

The "puffs" are not usually a problem, but something that can frighten an uninformed owner. This is a fairly frequent occurrence in all short-nosed breeds. Because of elongation of the soft palate, a dog suddenly draws in short, sharp breaths and looks very tense, often standing four square as he does so. This is usually brought on by a dog's becoming very excited, and usually only lasts a matter of seconds. Although this is not a major problem, it can be alarming and should always be investigated by the owner. There can be other reasons for such puffing. For example, a grass seed could be lodged in the nasal cavity and this would, of course, have to be removed at once.

UMBILICAL HERNIAS
A genetic problem common in the Pekingese is the occurrence of umbilical hernias. This occurs when a pup's umbilical ring does not close properly and a hole is left, allowing a bit of the intestine to poke through the wall of the abdomen. The skin is not ruptured, and usually the hernia is noticed as a lump on the pup's belly. The danger of an umbilical hernia depends on its severity; a small hole should not present a problem but, the larger the hole, the more of the intestine that can

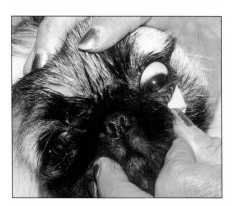

poke through and possibly twist.

Umbilical hernias can be corrected surgically. The condition is genetic, though, meaning that any Pekingese affected with an umbilical hernia should never be used for breeding, even if the umbilical hernia has been fixed surgically.

HEART PROBLEMS
Heart disease has been seen in the Pekingese, and this is not confined to only older dogs. However, there are many forms of heart disease and by no means are all inherited. Obviously, any sign of such disease should be checked out thoroughly by a vet, but of course many Pekingese live to ripe old ages with no heart problems at all.

EYES
Because of the breed's fairly prominent eyes, it is not difficult for a Peke to injure his eyes. Corneal ulceration is counted among the most common problems in the breed. An ulcer may be caused by a scratch, or even a knock that may have gone unnoticed. At the first sign of any eye trouble, you should contact your vet, because rapid action can result in complete recovery instead of impaired vision or even loss of sight.

Take special care that grass seeds, fluff or dust do not get embedded in the eye; an early

The Peke's prominent eyes require care and careful observation to be sure they have not been injured.

ENCHANTING NAMES

In his wonderful little book on the Pekingese, Clifford Hubbard was struck by people's choices of names. He noticed that Ping Pong and Pong Ping popped up time and time again. Other interesting names included Ping Suey and Minky Mog, but the name he thought "took the biscuit" was Wotton Pin-ta-lo-poh-lo-to-sho.

indicator that this may have happened is excessive watering from the eye.

Some Pekes suffer from dry eye, which can arise for a number of different reasons. If dry eye is suspected, your vet should examine your Peke's eyes. If the diagnosis is confirmed, he will be able to prescribe treatment to ease the problem.

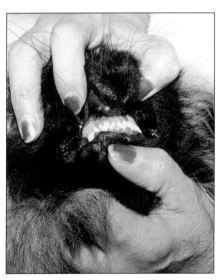

Like many small breeds, Pekes can start to lose their teeth at an early age. To preserve their teeth for as long as possible, dental hygiene should be practiced regularly.

LEGS

Many Toy dogs and other small breeds suffer from trouble with the knee joints, known as luxating patella. This is considered inherited in the Peke; thus, affected dogs shoud not be bred. It is important that a dog should not carry too much weight, as this is likely to make the problem worse. Many dogs with luxating patella live with this problem without experiencing pain, but surgery sometimes has to be considered and is often successful. Sometimes other joint diseases, such as osteoarthritis, can result from severe patellar luxation.

BACK PROBLEMS

The Pekingese is susceptible to back problems, with invertebral disk disease being one of the most common problems seen in the breed. This is a genetic degenerative disease of the disks, which connect the vertebrae of the spinal column. Thus, as the disks weaken, the back does not have as much support, causing pain, lameness and even paralysis in severe cases.

Owners should take preventative measures, whether or not their Pekes are genetically predisposed to back problems. These precautions include keeping the dog at a correct weight, as excess weight strains the back, and not allowing the dog to jump on and off of furniture or climb stairs.

If your Pekingese experiences back problems, there are many types of treatments available to make the dog as comfortable as possible. These range from therapeutic measures and medications to surgical treatments.

TEETH

As with many of the smaller breeds, some Pekingese lose their teeth at a relatively early age. It is therefore important to pay close attention to the care of teeth and gums so that they remain as healthy as possible, thereby preventing decay, infection and resultant loss.

Infection in the gums may not just stop there. The bacteria from the infection is carried through the bloodstream, the result of which can be disease of liver, kidney, heart and joints. This is all the more reason to realize that efficient dental care is of the utmost importance throughout a dog's life.

BAD BREATH

Offensive breath is usually the result of problems with teeth and gums, but it can also be caused by indigestion, or may sometimes be related to the kidneys. In cases of digestive problems' giving rise to bad breath, charcoal, either in the form of tablets or granules, can often help. A

DOGS, DOGS, GOOD FOR YOUR HEART!

People usually purchase dogs for companionship, but studies show that dogs can help to improve their owners' health and level of activity, as well as lower a human's risk of coronary heart disease. Without even realizing it, when a person puts time into exercising, grooming and feeding a dog, he also puts more time into his own personal health care. Dog owners establish more routine schedules for their dogs to follow, which can have positive effects on their own health. Dogs also teach us patience, offer unconditional love and provide the joy of having a furry friend to pet!

A Pekingese
"pack," enjoying
lap time with their
mistress in the
good old
summertime. Be
sure to protect
your short-faced
Peke during warm
weather.

A Pekingese "pack," enjoying lap time with their mistress in the good old summertime. Be sure to protect your short-faced Peke during warm weather.

useful aid to masking bad breath is the use of chlorophyll tablets.

GRASS SEEDS

Because they are low to the ground, and have long coats and long ears, Pekingese occasionally pick up grass seeds, the barbed ends of which can penetrate right into the skin. Often they are just picked up on the coat but work their way down to the skin, where they cause pain and sometimes abscesses. They can even get stuck inside the nostrils or between the pads of the feet. It is therefore always important to check the coat after a walk, particularly in late summer and autumn. At any sign of distress, the cause must be investigated immediately.

HEAT SENSITIVITY

Pekingese tend not to take well to hot temperatures, because of their profuse coats and their facial structure. Caution should therefore be taken never to exercise a Peke in excessive heat.

OTHER HEALTH PROBLEMS

It must be understood that there are many other health problems that can be suffered by dogs, but it is not possible to outline them all here. As you get to know your Pekingese, you will also come to recognize if he is ever "off color," at which time a quick trip to the vet can help to nip a problem in the bud so that suitable care may be given and the problem taken care of as quickly as possible.

PEKINGESE

In the USA, the breed standard for the Pekingese has been revised three times, in 1933, 1956 and, most recently, in 1995. The last is the most detailed to date and was submitted by the Pekingese Club of America Inc., and approved by the Board of Directors of the American Kennel Club (AKC) on June 13, 1995 becoming effective on July 31 of that year.

THE AKC STANDARD FOR THE PEKINGESE

REVISED STANDARD FOR THE PEKINGESE

The Board of Directors of the American Kennel Club has approved the following revised standard for the Pekingese as submitted by the Pekingese Club of America, Inc.

General Appearance: The Pekingese is a well-balanced, compact dog with heavy front and lighter hindquarters. It must suggest its Chinese origin in its directness, independence, individuality and expression. Its image is lionlike. It should imply courage, boldness and self-esteem rather than prettiness, daintiness or delicacy.

Size, Substance, Proportion: Size/Substance The Pekingese should be surprisingly heavy when lifted. It has a stocky, muscular body. The bone of the forequarters must be very heavy in relation to the size of the dog. All weights are correct within the limit of 14 pounds, provided that type and points are not sacrificed. *Disqualification*: Weight over 14 pounds. **Proportion** The length of the body, from the front of the

The standard calls for the Pekingese to possess a bold, lionlike appearance.

breast bone in a straight line to the buttocks, is slightly greater than the height at the withers. Overall balance is of utmost importance.

Head: Skull The topskull is massive, broad and flat (not dome-shaped). The topskull, the high, wide cheek bones, broad lower jaw and wide chin are the structural formation of the correctly shaped face. When viewed frontally, the skull is wider than deep and contributes

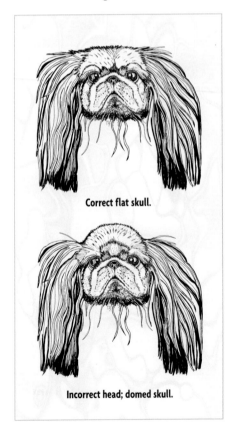

Correct flat skull.

Incorrect head; domed skull.

to the rectangular envelope-shaped appearance of the head. In profile, the Pekingese face must be flat. The chin, nose leather and brow all lie in one plane. In the natural position of the head, this plane appears vertical but slants very slightly backward from chin to forehead. **Nose** It is black, broad, very short and in profile, contributes to the flat appearance of the face. Nostrils are open. The nose is positioned between the eyes so that a line drawn horizontally across the top of the nose intersects the center of the eyes. **Eyes** They are large, very dark, round, lustrous and set wide apart. The look is bold, not bulging. The eye rims are black and the white of the eye does not show when the dog is looking straight ahead. **Wrinkle** It effectively separates the upper and lower areas of the face. The appearance is of a hair-covered fold of skin, extending from one cheek, over the bridge of the nose in a wide inverted "V," to the other cheek. It is *never* so prominent or heavy as to crowd the facial features nor to obscure a large portion of the eyes or the nose from view. **Stop** It is deep. The bridge of the nose is completely obscured from view by hair and/or the over-nose wrinkle. **Muzzle** This is very short and broad with high, wide cheek bones. The color of the skin is black. Whiskers add to the

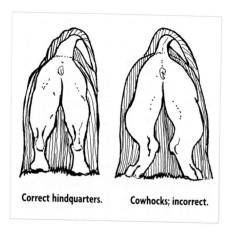

Correct hindquarters.   Cowhocks; incorrect.

Severely undershot bite with teeth showing when mouth is closed.

Oriental expression. **Mouth** The lower jaw is slightly undershot. The lips meet on a level plane and neither teeth nor tongue show when the mouth is closed. The lower jaw is strong, wide, firm and straight across at the chin. An excessively strong chin is as undesirable as a weak one. **Ears** They are heart-shaped and set on the front corners of the skull extending the line of the topskull. Correctly placed ears frame the sides of the face and with their heavy feathering create an illusion of additional width of the head. **Pigment** The skin of the nose, lips and eye rims is black on all colors.

Neck, Body, Tail: Neck It is very short, thick and set back into the shoulder. **Body** This is pear-shaped and compact. It is heavy in front with well-sprung ribs slung between the forelegs. The broad chest, with little or no protruding breast bone, tapers to lighter loins with a distinct waist. The topline is level. **Tail** The base is set high; the remainder is carried well over the center of the back. Long, profuse straight feathering may fall to either side.

Forequarters: They are short, thick and heavy-boned. The bones of the forelegs are slightly bowed between the pastern and elbow. Shoulders are gently laid back and fit smoothly into the body.

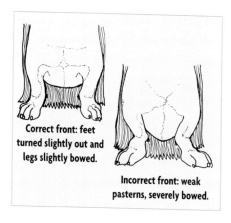

Correct front: feet turned slightly out and legs slightly bowed.

Incorrect front: weak pasterns, severely bowed.

The elbows are always close to the body. Front feet are large, flat and turned slightly out. The dog must stand well up on feet.

Hindquarters: They are lighter in bone than the forequarters. There is moderate angulation and definition of stifle and hock. When viewed from behind, the rear legs are reasonably close and parallel and the feet point straight ahead. **Soundness is essential in both forequarters and hindquarters.**

Coat: Body Coat It is full-bodied, with long, coarse textured, straight, stand-off coat and thick, softer undercoat. The coat forms a noticeable mane on the neck and shoulder area with the coat on the remainder of the body somewhat shorter in length. A long and profuse coat is desirable providing that it does not obscure the shapeliness of the body, nor sacrifice the correct coat texture. **Feathering** Long feathering is found on the back of the thighs and forelegs, and on the ears, tail and toes. The feathering is left on the toes but should not be so long as to prevent free movement. **Color:** All coat colors and markings, including parti-colors, are allowable and of equal merit.

Gait: The gait is unhurried and dignified, with a slight roll over the shoulders. The rolling gait is caused by the bowed front legs and heavier, wider forequarters pivoting on the tapered waist and the lighter, straight parallel hindquarters. The rolling motion is smooth and effortless and is as free as possible from bouncing, prancing or jarring.

Temperament: A combination of regal dignity, self-importance, self-confidence and exasperating stubbornness make for a good natured, lively and affectionate companion to those who have earned its respect.

Body outline of a sheared dog, compared to coated dog, to illustrate the body structure underneath the coat.

The foregoing is a description of the ideal Pekingese. Any deviation should be penalized in direct proportion to the extent of that deviation.

Faults to be noted:
Dudley, liver or gray nose.
Brown, yellow or blue eyes.
Protruding tongue or teeth.
Overshot upper jaw.
Wry mouth.
Ears set much too high, low or far back.
Roach or swayback.
Straight-boned forelegs.

Disqualification: Weight over 14 pounds.

Approved June 13, 1995
Effective July 31, 1995

COMMENTS ON THE STANDARD

The foregoing standard is effectively a "blueprint" for the breed, setting down the various points of the dog in words, enabling the reader to conjure up a mental picture of the ideal representative of the breed. However, this is more easily said than done. Not only do standards vary from country to country, but people's interpretations of breed standards vary also. It is this difference of interpretation that causes different judges to select different dogs for top honors, for their opinions differ as to which

Points:	
Expression	5
Nose	5
Stop	5
Muzzle	5
Legs and Feet	15
Tail	5
Skull	10
Eyes	5
Ears	5
Shape of Body	20
Coat, Feather & Condition	10
Action	10
Total	**100**

dog most closely fits the breed standard. That is not to say that a good dog does not win regularly under different judges, nor that an inferior dog may rarely even be placed at a show, at least not among quality competition.

Although they had a similar basis, today there are considerable variances between the British and American standards, with the latter being considerably more detailed, especially in relation to the head. It will be noted that, in the AKC standard, the word "massive" is used to describe the topskull, whereas the English standard says that the head should be large. The reason for this is that the English Kennel Club has disallowed use of the word "massive," so as to discourage whelping problems.

In the AKC standard, the nostrils are to be open, while the British breed standard calls for them to be large and open. These statements in both standards are included for more than purely esthetic reasons, for it is important in a short-nosed breed that breathing problems are not encouraged.

In America, the weight limit is higher than that in Britain, where the standard reads: "Ideal weight not exceeding 5 kg (11 lb) for dogs and 5.4 kg (12 lb) for bitches. Dogs should look small but be surprisingly heavy when picked up; heavy bone and a sturdy well-built body are essentials of the breed." However, the weight specification in the US is indeed strict, for exhibits exceeding the maximum weight are disqualified from competition.

Another very significant difference is that the AKC lists individual "Faults to be Noted," whereas The Kennel Club does not allow faults to be listed in "any breed standard. A standard clause included in every breed's standard reads: "Faults: Any departure from the foregoing points should be considered a fault and the seriousness with which the fault should be regarded should be in exact proportion to its degree." The American list of points for the various aspects of the Pekingese is also of interest, for this is a good indicator of how much stress breeders and judges should place on various parts of the breed's makeup.

Although a great deal can be learned from the breed standard, only by seeing good-quality, typical specimens can one really learn to appreciate the breed's many merits. Close observation of the breed also enables one to recognize untypicalities when they occur. Therefore, readers interested in showing their Pekingese should watch other dogs being exhibited, and learn as much as possible from established breeders and exhibitors. It is sensible to attend breed seminars, often hosted by breed clubs, in which the finer points of the breed can be explained fully and discussed. There is usually a dog, or perhaps several, available for demonstration purposes, and there may even be an opportunity for participants to feel beneath the coat for the structure of the animal.

If a Pekingese is well constructed, not only can this be seen in the dog's typical movement but also in the breed's very special outline, which can be observed from every angle. This is a veritable joy to the eye of a Pekingese devotee, as is the breed's remarkable character, which cannot fail to shine through.

PEKINGESE

You have probably decided on a Pekingese as your choice of pet following a visit to the home of a friend or acquaintance, where you saw a somewhat stately Peke, rolling politely around the house, wearing a majestic coat. Or maybe the Peke looked thoroughly endearing while "dancing" on his hind legs, something rather characteristic of the breed. However, as a potential owner, you must realize that a good deal of care, commitment and careful training goes into raising a boisterous puppy so that your pet turns into a well-behaved, dignified adult.

In deciding to take on a new Peke puppy, you will be committing yourself to many years of responsibility. No dog should be discarded after a few months, or even a few years, after the novelty has worn off. Instead, your Pekingese should be joining your household to spend the rest of his days with you, so you should bear in mind that a healthy Pekingese usually lives between 12 and 14 years.

Although temperamentally a Pekingese is easier to look after than many other breeds, you will still need to carry out a certain amount of training. You will need to take a firm but gentle approach in order to get the very best out of

PUPPY PERSONALITY

When a litter becomes available to you, choosing a pup out of all those adorable faces will not be an easy task! Sound temperament is of utmost importance, but each pup has its own personality and some may be better suited to you than others. A feisty, independent pup will do well in a home with older children and adults, while quiet, shy puppies will thrive in homes with minimal noise and distractions. Your breeder knows the pups best and should be able to guide you in the right direction.

Adding a Peke to your life means over a decade of canine companionship with this most regal and charming breed.

large dog, there will undoubtedly be a period of settling in. This will be great fun, but you must be prepared for mishaps around the home during the first few weeks of your life together. It will be important that precious ornaments are kept well out of harm's way, and you will have to think twice about where you place hot cups of coffee or anything breakable. Accidents can and do happen, so you will need to think ahead so as to avoid these.

your pet, which is a representative of a strong-willed breed. Because of this, you must make it eminently clear from the very beginning that your dog is to do as you command.

Regarding cleanliness around the home, you will need to teach your puppy what is and is not expected. You will need to be consistent in your instructions; it is no good accepting certain behavior one day and not the next. Not only will your puppy simply not understand, he will be utterly confused. Your Peke will want to please you, so you will need to demonstrate clearly how your puppy is to achieve this.

Although the dog you are taking into your home will be small, and therefore probably less troublesome in many ways than a

ARE YOU PREPARED?

Unfortunately, when a puppy is bought by someone who does not take into consideration the time and attention that dog ownership requires, it is the puppy who suffers when he is either abandoned or placed in a shelter by a frustrated owner. So all of the "homework" you do in preparation for your pup's arrival will benefit you both. The more informed you are, the more you will know what to expect and the better equipped you will be to handle the ups and downs of raising a puppy. Hopefully, everyone in the household is willing to do his part in raising and caring for the pup. The anticipation of owning a dog often brings a lot of promises from excited family members: "I will walk him every day," "I will feed him," "I will housebreak him," etc., but these things take time and effort, and promises can easily be forgotten once the novelty of the new pet has worn off.

Before making your commitment to a new puppy, do also think carefully about your future vacation plans. Depending on where you wish to travel, your dog may or may not be able to accompany you. If you have thought things through carefully, and have discussed the matter thoroughly with all members of your family, hopefully you will

BOY OR GIRL?

An important consideration to be discussed is the sex of your puppy. For a family companion, a bitch may be the better choice, considering the female's inbred concern for all young creatures and her accompanying tolerance and patience. It is always advisable to spay a pet female or neuter a pet male, as this may guarantee your Peke a longer life.

The health and soundness of the puppy are the first considerations for the potential owner. These characteristics should be evident in all pups in the litter.

TEMPERAMENT COUNTS

Your selection of a good puppy can be determined by your needs. A show potential or a good pet? It is your choice. Every puppy, however, should be of good temperament. Although show-quality puppies are bred and raised with emphasis on physical conformation, responsible breeders strive for equally good temperament. Do not buy from a breeder who concentrates solely on physical beauty at the expense of personality.

have come to the right decision. If you decide that a Pekingese should join your family, this will hopefully be a happy, long-term relationship for all parties concerned.

SELECTING A PEKE PUPPY
Although you may be looking for a Pekingese as a pet rather than a show dog, this does not mean that you want a dog that is in any way "second-rate." A caring breeder raises the entire litter of puppies with the same amount of dedication, and a puppy destined for a pet home should be just as healthy and sound as one destined for the show ring.

Because you have carefully selected this breed, you will want a Peke that is a typical specimen, both in looks and in temperament. In your endeavors to find such a puppy, you will have to select the breeder with care. The American Kennel Club and the Pekingese Club of America will be able to give you names of reputable contacts. These people can put you in touch with breeders, with whom you can discuss your interest in buying a puppy. However, although they can point you in the right direction, it will be up to you to do your homework and choose your breeder carefully.

Even though you are probably not looking for a show dog, it is always a good idea to visit a

INHERIT THE MIND

In order to know whether or not a puppy will fit into your lifestyle, you need to assess his personality. A good way to do this is to interact with his parents. Your pup inherits not only his appearance but also his personality and temperament from the sire and dam. If the parents are fearful or overly aggressive, these same traits may likely show up in your puppy.

show so that you can see quality specimens of the breed. This will also give you an opportunity to meet breeders, who should be able to answer some of your queries. In addition, you will get some idea about which breeders appear to take most care of their stock, and which are likely to have given their puppies the best possible start in life.

When buying your puppy, you will need to know about vaccinations, those already given and those still due. It is important that you provide your chosen vet with documentation from the breeder to prove this, so that he can continue with an appropriate vaccination schedule. A worming routine is also vital for any young puppy, so the breeder should be able to tell you exactly what treatment has been given, when it has been administered and how you should continue.

Clearly when selecting a puppy, the one you choose must be in good condition. The coat should look healthy and there should be no discharge from eyes or nose. Ears should also be clean, and, of course, there should be absolutely no sign of parasites. Check that there is no rash on the skin, and of course the puppy you choose should not have evidence of loose motions. Also check to see if dewclaws have been removed.

When visiting the breeder, take a look around the premises and meet all of the dogs. This will be a good indicator of how dogs of the breeder's line mature and how well he looks after them.

PEDIGREE VS. REGISTRATION CERTIFICATE

Too often new owners are confused between these two important documents. Your puppy's pedigree, essentially a family tree, is a written record of a dog's genealogy of three generations or more. The pedigree will show you the names as well as performance titles of all dogs in your pup's background. Your breeder must provide you with a registration application, with his part properly filled out. You must complete the application and send it to the AKC with the proper fee. Every puppy must come from a litter that has been AKC-registered by the breeder, born in the US and from a sire and dam that are also registered with the AKC.

The seller must provide you with complete records to identify the puppy. The AKC requires that the seller provide the buyer with the following: breed; sex, color and markings; date of birth; litter number (when available); names and registration numbers of the parents; breeder's name; and date sold or delivered.

You will be able to visit the litter before the pups are old enough to go home and possibly to select your pup at that time. The breeder will then keep your pup until he is old enough to go home with you. Most breeders wait until the pups are around 12 weeks old to release them, *never* before eight weeks.

Be sure, too, that if you decide to buy a puppy, all relevant documentation is provided at the time of sale. You will need a copy of the pedigree, American Kennel Club registration documents, vaccination certificates and a feeding chart so that you know exactly how the puppy has been fed and how you should continue. Some breeders provide their puppy-buyers with a small amount of food. This prevents the risk of an upset tummy, allowing for a gradual change of diet if that particular brand of food is not locally available.

COMMITMENT OF OWNERSHIP

After considering all of these factors, you have most likely already made some very important decisions about selecting your Pekingese puppy. If you have selected a breeder, you have gone a step further—you have done your research and found a responsible, conscientious person who breeds quality Pekingese and who should be a reliable source of help as you and your

ARE YOU A FIT OWNER?
If the breeder from whom you are buying a puppy asks you a lot of personal questions, do not be insulted. Such a breeder wants to be sure that you will be a fit provider for the Peke throughout the dog's life.

playful, friendly, aggressive, etc. Equally as important, you will learn to recognize what a healthy pup should look and act like. All of these things will help you in your search, and when you find the Pekingese that was meant for you, you will know it!

Researching your breed, selecting a responsible breeder and observing as many pups as possible are all important steps on the way to dog ownership. It may seem like a lot of effort...and you have not even brought the pup home yet! Buying a puppy is not—or *should* not be—just another whimsical purchase. This is one instance in which you actually do get to choose your own family! You may be thinking that buying a puppy should be fun—it should not be so serious and so much work. Keep in mind that your puppy is not a cuddly stuffed toy or table ornament, but a creature that will become a real member of your family. You will

Your home will be a big new world for your tiny Peke puppy to explore. Ensure a safe environment and give him time to become adjusted.

puppy adjust to life together.

Even if you have not yet found the Pekingese puppy of your dreams, observing litters will help you learn to recognize certain behavior and to determine what a pup's behavior indicates about his temperament. You will be able to pick out which pups are the leaders, which ones are less outgoing, which ones are confident, which ones are shy,

Crate training offers the Peke owner many advantages, including assistance in toilet training, safety during travel and a convenient, secure place for the dog to retreat at busy times.

Crate training offers the Peke owner many advantages, including assistance in toilet training, safety during travel and a convenient, secure place for the dog to retreat at busy times.

come to realize that, while buying a puppy is a pleasurable and exciting endeavor, it is not something to be taken lightly. Relax…
the fun will start when the pup comes home!

Always keep in mind that a puppy is nothing more than a baby in a furry disguise…a baby who is virtually helpless in a human world and who trusts his owner for fulfillment of his basic needs for survival. In addition to food, water and shelter, your pup needs care, protection, guidance and love. If you are not prepared to commit to this, then you are not prepared to own a dog.

"Wait a minute," you say. "How hard could this be? All of my neighbors own dogs and they seem to be doing just fine. Why should I have to worry about all of this?" Well, you should not worry about it; in fact, you will probably find that once your Pekingese pup gets used to his new home, he will fall into his place in the family quite naturally. But it never hurts to emphasize the commitment of dog ownership. With some time and patience, it is really not too difficult to raise a curious and exuberant Pekingese pup to be a well-adjusted and well-mannered adult dog—a dog that could be your most loyal friend.

PREPARING PUPPY'S PLACE IN YOUR HOME
Researching your breed and finding a breeder are only two aspects of the "homework" you will have to do before bringing

your Pekingese puppy home. You will also have to prepare your home and family for the new addition. Much as you would prepare a nursery for a newborn baby, you will need to designate a place in your home that will be the puppy's own. How you prepare your home will depend on how much freedom the dog will be allowed. Whatever you decide, you must ensure that he has a place that he can "call his own."

When you bring your new puppy into your home, you are bringing him into what will become his home as well. Obviously, you did not buy a puppy so that he could take control of

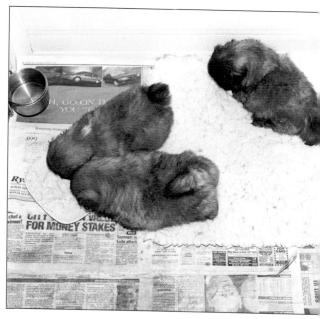

YOUR SCHEDULE . . .
If you lead an erratic, unpredictable life, with daily or weekly changes in your work requirements, consider the problems of owning a puppy. The new puppy has to be fed regularly, socialized (loved, petted, handled, introduced to other people) and, most importantly, allowed to go outdoors to relieve himself. As the dog gets older, he can be more tolerant of deviations in his feeding and toilet schedule.

your home, but in order for a puppy to grow into a stable, well-adjusted dog, he has to feel comfortable in his surroundings. Remember, he is leaving the warmth and security of his mother and littermates, as well as the familiarity of the only place he has ever known, so it is important to make his transition as easy as possible. By preparing a place in your home for the puppy, you are making him feel as welcome as possible in a strange new place. It should not take him long to get used to it, but the sudden shock of being transplanted is somewhat traumatic for a young pup. Imagine how a small child would feel in the same situation—that is how

The breeder starts his pups off with good nutrition and will be a valuable source of help regarding how best to continue feeding your puppy.

CRATE-TRAINING TIPS

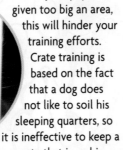

During the housebreaking process, if your pup is given too big an area, this will hinder your training efforts. Crate training is based on the fact that a dog does not like to soil his sleeping quarters, so it is ineffective to keep a pup in a crate that is so big that he can eliminate in one end and get far enough away from it to sleep. Since Pekes do not require large crates, this should not pose a problem. Also, you want to make the crate den-like for the pup. Blankets and a favorite toy will make the crate cozy for the small pup; as he grows, you may want to evict some of his "roommates" to make more room. It will take some coaxing at first, but be patient. Given some time to get used to it, your pup will adapt to his new home-within-a-home quite nicely.

not the case at all. More breeders and trainers are recommending crates as a preferred tool for pet puppies as well as for show puppies. Crates are not cruel—crates have many humane and highly effective uses in dog care and training. For example, crate training is a very popular and very successful housebreaking method. A crate can keep your dog safe during travel and, perhaps most importantly, a crate provides your dog with a place of his own in your home. It serves as a "doggie bedroom" of sorts—your Pekingese can curl up in his crate when he wants to sleep or when he just needs a break. Many dogs sleep in their crates overnight. When lined with soft bedding and with a favorite toy inside, a crate becomes a cozy pseudo-den for your dog. Like his ancestors, he too will seek out the comfort and retreat of a den—you just happen to be providing him with something a little more luxurious than what his early ancestors enjoyed.

As far as purchasing a crate,

your puppy must be feeling. It is up to you to reassure him and to let him know, "Little lion dog, you are going to like it here!"

WHAT YOU SHOULD BUY

CRATE

To someone unfamiliar with the use of crates in dog training, it may seem like punishment to shut a dog in a crate, but this is

Pekes love toys. Be sure to get toys made especially for dogs, as these will be the safest for the Peke to enjoy.

the type that you buy is up to you. It will most likely be one of the two most popular types: wire or fiberglass. There are advantages and disadvantages to each type. For example, a wire crate is more open, allowing the air to flow through and affording the dog a view of what is going on around him, while a fiberglass crate is sturdier. Both can double as travel crates, providing protection for the dog in the car. A small crate will easily accommodate a Pekingese puppy or adult.

BEDDING

A crate pad in the dog's crate will help the dog feel more at home, and you may also like to give him a small blanket. These will take the place of the leaves, twigs, etc., that the pup would use in the wild to make a den; the pup can make his own "burrow" in the crate. Although your pup is far removed from his den-making ancestors, the denning instinct is still a part of his genetic makeup. Second, until you bring your pup home, he has been sleeping amid the warmth of his mother and littermates, and while a blanket is not the same as a warm, breathing body, it still provides heat and something with which to snuggle. You will want to wash your pup's bedding frequently in case he has an accident in his crate, and replace or remove any blanket or

STRESS-FREE
Some experts in canine health advise that stress during a dog's early years of development can compromise and weaken his immune system, and may trigger the potential for a shortened life. They emphasize the need for happy and stress-free growing-up years.

padding that becomes worn and starts to fall apart.

TOYS

Toys are a must for dogs of all ages, especially for curious playful pups. Puppies are the "children" of the dog world, and what child does not love toys? Chew toys provide enjoyment to both dog and owner—your dog will enjoy playing with his favorite toys, while you will enjoy the fact that they distract him from your expensive shoes and leather sofa. Puppies love to chew; in fact, chewing is a physical need for pups as they are teething, and everything looks appetizing! The full range of your possessions—

TOYS, TOYS, TOYS!

With a big variety of dog toys available, and so many that look like they would be a lot of fun for a dog, be careful in your selection. It is amazing what a set of puppy teeth can do to an innocent-looking toy; so, obviously, safety is a major consideration. Be sure to choose the most durable products that you can find. Hard nylon bones and toys are a safe bet, and many of them are offered in different scents and flavors that will be sure to capture your dog's attention. Strong nylon rope toys are also popular; dogs enjoy chewing on them and they have the added benefit of "flossing" the teeth as the dog chews.

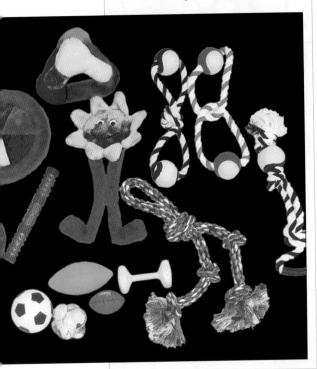

from bedroom slippers to Oriental rug—are fair game in the eyes of a teething pup. Puppies are not all that discerning when it comes to finding something to literally "sink their teeth into"—everything tastes great!

Pekingese puppies, due to their short noses and mouths, should not be offered balls. Flat toys are more easily picked up and enjoyed. Be sure that all dog toys are safe and of the highest quality available. Breeders advise owners to resist stuffed toys, because they can become de-stuffed in no time. Similarly, squeaky toys are quite popular and can be used as an aid in training, but not for free play. If a pup "disembowels" one of these, the small plastic squeaker inside can be dangerous if swallowed. Monitor the condition of all your pup's toys carefully and get rid of any that have been chewed to the point of becoming potentially dangerous.

Be careful of natural bones, which have a tendency to splinter into sharp, dangerous pieces. Also be careful of rawhide, which can turn into pieces that are easy to swallow or a mushy mess on your carpet.

LEASH

A nylon leash is probably the best option, as it is the most resistant to puppy teeth should your pup take a liking to chewing

CHOOSE AN APPROPRIATE COLLAR

The **BUCKLE COLLAR** is the standard collar used for everyday purposes. Be sure that you adjust the buckle on growing puppies. Check it every day. It can become too tight overnight! These collars can be made of leather or nylon. Attach your dog's identification tags to this collar.

The **CHOKE COLLAR** is designed for training. It is constructed of highly polished steel so that it slides easily through the stainless steel loop. The idea is that the dog controls the pressure around his neck and he will stop pulling if the collar becomes uncomfortable. Since it should *not* be used on coated breeds or small breeds, it is doubly unsuitable for the Pekingese.

The **HALTER** is for a trained dog that has to be restrained to prevent running away, chasing a cat and the like. Considered the most humane of all collars, it is frequently used on smaller dogs on which collars are not comfortable.

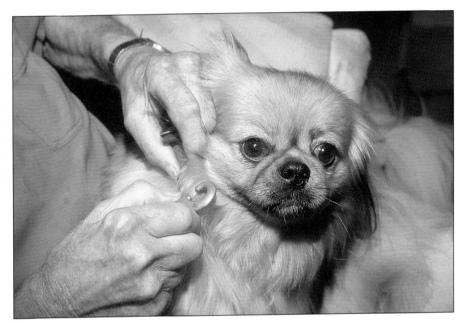

on his leash. Of course, this is a habit that should be nipped in the bud, but if your pup likes to chew on his leash he has a very slim chance of being able to chew through the strong nylon. Nylon leashes are also lightweight, which is good for a young Pekingese who is just getting used to the idea of walking on a leash. For everyday walking and safety purposes, the nylon leash is a good choice. As your pup grows up and gets used to walking on the leash, you may want to purchase a flexible leash. These leashes allow you to extend the length to give the dog a broader area to explore or to shorten the length to keep the dog close to you.

COLLAR

Your pup should get used to wearing a collar, since you will want to attach his ID tags to it and you will need the collar and leash for walks and training. A lightweight nylon collar is a good choice; make sure that it fits snugly enough so that the pup cannot wriggle out of it, but is loose enough so that it will not be uncomfortably tight around the pup's neck. You should be able to fit a finger between the pup and the collar. It may take some time for your pup to get used to wearing the collar, but soon he will not even notice that it is there. Be certain that the collar is not damaging to the Pekingese's coat. Since your Pekingese should spend most of his time indoors, you may wish only to attach the collar while he is outdoors.

FOOD AND WATER BOWLS
Your pup will need two bowls, one for food and one for water. Stainless steel or sturdy plastic bowls are popular choices. Many types are available at pet shops. Your Peke will require only small-sized bowls. Purchase durable bowls that can be cleaned easily.

CLEANING SUPPLIES
Until a pup is housebroken, you will be doing a lot of cleaning. "Accidents" will occur, which is okay in the beginning because the puppy does not know any better. All you can do is be prepared to clean up any accidents. Old rags, paper towels, newspapers and a safe disinfectant are good to have on hand.

BEYOND THE BASICS
The items previously discussed are the bare necessities. You will find out what else you need as you go along—grooming supplies, flea/tick protection, baby gates to partition a room, etc. These things will vary depending on your situation, but it is important that right away you have everything you need to feed and make your Pekingese comfortable in his first few days at home.

FINANCIAL RESPONSIBILITY
Grooming tools, collars, leashes, a crate, a dog bed and, of course, toys will be expenses to you when you first obtain your pup, and the cost will continue throughout your dog's lifetime. If your puppy damages or destroys your possessions (as most puppies surely will!) or something belonging to a neighbor, you can calculate additional expense. There is also flea and pest control, which every dog owner faces more than once. You must be able to handle the financial responsibility of owning a dog.

Be a good citizen and clean up after your dog.

PUPPY-PROOFING
YOUR HOME

Aside from making sure that your Pekingese will be comfortable in your home, you also have to make sure that your home is safe for your Pekingese. This means taking precautions that your pup will not get into anything he should not get into and that there is nothing within his reach that may harm him should he sniff it, chew it, inspect it, etc. This probably seems obvious since, while you are primarily concerned with your pup's safety, at the same time you do not want your belongings to be ruined.

Breakables should be placed out of reach if your dog is to have full run of the house. If he is to be limited to certain places within the house, keep any potentially dangerous items in the "off-limits" areas. An electrical wire can pose a danger should the puppy decide to taste it, so all wires and cords should be fastened tightly against the wall and away from puppy teeth. If your dog is going to spend time in a crate, make sure that there is nothing near his crate that he can reach if he sticks his curious little paws through the openings. Just as you would with a child, keep all household cleaners and chemicals where the pup cannot reach them.

It is also important to make sure that the outside of your home is safe. Of course your puppy should never be unsupervised, but a pup let loose in the yard will want to walk around and explore, and he should be granted that freedom. Do not let a fence give you a false sense of security; you would be surprised how crafty (and persistent) a dog can be in working out how to dig under and squeeze his way through small holes. Be sure that the fence is well embedded into the ground and look out for any gaps in the fence that need repair. It doesn't require a large gap for the Pekingese to slip through. Fortunately, the Pekingese cannot jump and climb as readily as many other dogs, and he likely won't be spending too much time outdoors to devise ways to

---

HOW VACCINES WORK

If you've just bought a puppy, you surely know the importance of having your pup vaccinated, but do you understand how vaccines work? Vaccines contain the same bacteria or viruses that cause the disease you want to prevent, but they have been chemically modified so that they don't cause any harm. Instead, the vaccine causes your dog to produce antibodies that fight the harmful bacteria. Thus, if your dog is exposed to the disease in the future, the antibodies will destroy the viruses or bacteria.

escape. Nonetheless, check the fence periodically to ensure that it is in good shape.

FIRST TRIP TO THE VET

You have picked out your puppy, and your home and family are ready. Now all you have to do is collect your Pekingese from the breeder and the fun begins, right? Well…not so fast. Something else you need to prepare is your pup's first trip to the veterinarian. Perhaps the breeder can recommend someone in the area that specializes in Toy dogs or brachycephalic breeds, or maybe you know some other Pekingese owners who can suggest a good vet. Either way, you should have an appointment arranged for your pup before you pick him up and plan to take him for an examination before bringing him home.

The pup's first visit will consist of an overall examination to make sure that the pup does not have any problems that are not apparent to you. The veterinarian will also set up a schedule for the pup's vaccinations; the breeder will tell you which ones the pup has already received and the vet can continue from there.

INTRODUCTION TO THE FAMILY

Everyone in the house will be excited about the puppy's coming home and will want to pet him and play with him, but it is best

TOXIC PLANTS

Examine your grass and landscaping before bringing your puppy home. Many varieties of plants have leaves, stems or flowers that are toxic if ingested, and you can depend on a curious puppy to investigate them. Ask your vet for information on poisonous plants or research them at your library.

If you see your dog carrying a piece of vegetation in his mouth, approach him in a quiet, disinterested manner, avoid eye contact, pet him and gradually remove the plant from his mouth. Alternatively, offer him a treat and maybe he'll drop the plant on his own accord. Be sure no toxic plants are growing in your yard or kept in your home.

CHEMICAL TOXINS
Scour your garage for potential puppy dangers. Remove weed killers, pesticides and antifreeze materials. Antifreeze is highly toxic and just a few drops can kill a puppy or an adult dog. The sweet taste attracts the animal, who will quickly consume it from the floor or pavement.

to make the introductions low-key so as not to overwhelm the puppy. He is apprehensive already. It is the first time he has been separated from his mother and the breeder, and the ride to your home is likely to be the first time he has been in a car. The last thing you want to do is smother him, as this will only frighten him further. This is not to say that human contact is not extremely necessary at this stage, because this is the time when a connection between the pup and his human family is formed. Gentle petting and soothing words should help console him, as well as just putting him down and letting him explore on his own (under your watchful eye, of course).

The pup may approach the family members or may busy himself with exploring for a while. Gradually, each person should spend some time with the pup, one at a time, crouching down to get as close to the pup's level as possible, letting him sniff their hands and petting him gently. The pup definitely needs human attention and he needs to be touched—this is how to form an immediate bond. Just remember that the pup is experiencing a lot of things for the first time, at the same time. There are new people, new noises, new smells, and new things to investigate, so be gentle, be affectionate and be as comforting as you can be.

YOUR PUP'S FIRST NIGHT HOME

You have traveled home with your new charge safely in his crate or on a passenger's lap. He's been to the vet for a thorough check-up; he's been weighed, his papers examined; perhaps he's even been vaccinated and wormed as well. He's met the whole family, including the excited children and the less-than-happy cat. He's explored his area, his new bed, the yard and anywhere else he's been permitted. He's eaten his first meal at home and relieved himself in the proper place. He's heard lots of new sounds, smelled new friends and seen more of the outside world than ever before.

That was just the first day! He's worn out and is ready for bed...or so you think!

It's puppy's first night and you are ready to say "Good

The Pekingese and the child are a natural pair, but the child must learn to respect the puppy's needs and limitations, and to always handle with care.

night"—keep in mind that this is puppy's first night ever to be sleeping alone. His dam and littermates are no longer at paw's length and he's a bit scared, cold and lonely. Be reassuring to your new family member, but this is not the time to spoil him and give in to his inevitable whining.

Puppies whine. They whine to let others know where they are and hopefully to get company out of it. Place your pup in his new bed or crate in his room and close the crate door. Mercifully, he may fall asleep without a sound. When the inevitable occurs, ignore the whining; he is fine. Be strong and keep his interest in mind. Do not allow yourself to become guilty and visit the pup. He will fall asleep.

SKULL & CROSSBONES

Thoroughly puppy-proof your house before bringing your puppy home. Never use cockroach or rodent poisons or plant fertilizers in any area accessible to the puppy. Avoid the use of toilet cleaners. Most dogs are born with "toilet-bowl sonar" and will take a drink if the lid is left open. Also keep the trash secured and out of reach.

Many breeders recommend placing a piece of bedding from the pup's former home in his new bed so that he recognizes the scent of his littermates. Others still advise placing a hot water bottle in his bed for warmth. This latter may be a good idea provided the pup doesn't attempt to suckle—he'll get good and wet

A soft snuggly bed will give your Peke pup a place to feel cozy and secure.

Too much too soon can make a Peke puppy want to hide! Don't overwhelm your puppy when introducing him to his new home. Take it slow and be reassuring.

and may not fall asleep so fast.

Puppy's first night can be somewhat stressful for the pup and his new family. Remember that you are setting the tone of nighttime at your house. Unless you want to play with your pup every night at 10 p.m., midnight and 2 a.m., don't initiate the habit. Your family will thank you, and soon so will your pup!

PREVENTING PUPPY PROBLEMS

SOCIALIZATION

Now that you have done all of the preparatory work and have helped your pup get accustomed to his new home and family, it is about time for you to have some fun! Socializing your Pekingese

pup gives you the opportunity to show off your new friend, and your pup gets to reap the benefits of being an adorable furry creature that people will want to pet and, in general, think is absolutely precious!

Besides getting to know his

PUP MEETS WORLD

Thorough socialization includes not only meeting new people but also being introduced to new experiences such as riding in the car, having his coat brushed, hearing the television, walking in a crowd—the list is endless. The more your pup experiences, and the more positive the experiences are, the less of a shock and the less frightening it will be for your pup to encounter new things.

new family, your puppy should be exposed to other people, animals and situations, but of course he must not come into close contact with dogs you don't know well until his course of injections is fully complete. Socialization will help him become well adjusted as he grows up and less prone to being timid or fearful of the new things he will encounter. Your pup's social-ization began at the breeder's, but now it is your responsibility to continue it. The socialization he receives in the first weeks after coming home is the most critical, as this is the time when he forms his impressions of the outside

PUPPY PROBLEMS

The majority of problems that are commonly seen in young pups will disappear as your dog gets older. However, how you deal with problems when he is young will determine how he reacts to discipline as an adult dog. It is important to establish who is boss (hopefully it will be you!) right away when you are first bonding with your dog. This bond will set the tone for the rest of your life together.

world. The eight-to-ten-week period, also known as the fear period, can be the Pekingese's most delicate time period. If you

Why wouldn't a "lion dog" welcome a feline friend? A puppy and kitten introduced to each other as youngsters often grow up to be the best of pals.

Many owners find it hard to own just one Peke! Socialization is exponentially important in multi-dog households, whether the dogs all grow up together or come into the home at different times.

have your Pekingese at this young age, be sure that you are reassuring and gentle. Lack of socialization can manifest itself in fear and aggression as the dog grows up. He needs lots of human contact, affection,

MANNERS MATTER

During the socialization process, a puppy should meet people, experience different environments and definitely be exposed to other canines. Through playing and interacting with other dogs, your puppy will learn lessons, ranging from controlling the pressure of his jaws by biting his littermates to the inner-workings of the canine pack that he will apply to his human relationships for the rest of his life. That is why removing a puppy from the litter too early (before eight weeks) can be detrimental to the pup's development.

handling and exposure to dogs and other kinds of pets.

Once your pup has received his necessary vaccinations, feel free to take him out and about (on his leash, of course). Walk him around the neighborhood, take him on your daily errands, let people pet him, let him meet other dogs and pets, etc. Puppies do not have to try to make friends; there will be no shortage of people who will want to introduce themselves. Just make sure that you carefully supervise each meeting. If the neighborhood children want to say hello, for example, that is great—children and pups most often make great companions. However, sometimes an excited child can unintentionally handle a pup too roughly, or an overzealous pup can playfully nip a little too hard. You want to make socialization experiences positive ones. What a pup learns during this very formative stage will affect his attitude toward future encounters. You want your dog to be comfortable around everyone. A pup that has a bad experience with a child may grow up to be a dog that is shy around or aggressive toward children that he meets later in life.

TRAINING TIP

Training your puppy takes much patience and can be frustrating at times, but you should see results from your efforts. If you have a puppy that seems untrainable, take him to a trainer or behaviorist. The dog may have a personality problem that requires the help of a professional, or perhaps you need help in learning how to train your dog.

Training a dog means setting boundaries to encourage good behavior and ensure the dog's safety. Gates designed for toddlers are equally effective in keeping dogs in their designated areas in the home.

CONSISTENCY IN TRAINING

Dogs, being pack animals, naturally need a leader, or else they try to establish dominance in their packs. When you bring a dog into your family, the choice of who becomes the leader and who becomes the "pack" is entirely up to you! Your pup's intuitive quest for dominance, coupled with the fact that it is nearly impossible to look at an adorable Pekingese pup, with his dark "puppy-dog" eyes and noble expression, and not cave in, give the pup almost an unfair advantage in getting the upper hand!

A pup will definitely test the waters to see what he can and cannot do. Do not give in to those pleading eyes—stand your ground when it comes to disciplining the pup and make sure that all family members do the same. Avoid discrepancies by having all members of the household decide on the rules before the pup even comes home...and be consistent in enforcing them! Early training shapes the dog's personality, so you cannot be unclear in what you expect.

COMMON PUPPY PROBLEMS

The best way to prevent puppy problems is to be proactive in stopping an undesirable behavior as soon as it starts. The old saying "You can't teach an old dog new tricks" does not necessarily hold true, but it *is* true that

> ### THE COCOA WARS
> Chocolate contains the chemical thebromine, which is poisonous to dogs, although "chocolates" especially made for dogs are safe (as they don't actually contain chocolate) but not recommended. Any item that encourages your dog to enjoy the taste of cocoa should be discouraged. You should also exercise caution when using mulch in your yard and garden. This frequently contains cocoa hulls, and dogs have been known to die from eating mulch.

it is much easier to discourage bad behavior in a young developing pup than to wait until the pup's bad behavior becomes the adult dog's bad habit. There are some problems that are especially prevalent in puppies as they develop.

NIPPING

As puppies start to teethe, they feel the need to sink their teeth into anything available...unfortunately that includes your fingers, arms, hair and toes. You may find this behavior cute for the first five seconds...until you feel just how sharp those puppy teeth are. This is something you want to discourage immediately and consistently with a firm "No!" (or whatever number of firm "Nos" it takes for him to understand that you mean business). Then

CHEWING TIPS

Chewing goes hand in hand with nipping in the sense that a teething puppy is always looking for a way to soothe his aching gums. In this case, instead of chewing on you, he may have taken a liking to your favorite shoe or something else that he should not be chewing. Again, realize that this is a normal canine behavior that does not need to be discouraged, only redirected. Your pup just needs to be taught what is acceptable to chew on and what is off-limits.

Consistently tell him "No!" when you catch him chewing on something forbidden and give him a chew toy. Conversely, praise him when you catch him chewing on something appropriate. In this way, you are discouraging the inappropriate behavior and reinforcing the desired behavior. The puppy's chewing should stop after his adult teeth have come in, but an adult dog continues to chew for various reasons—perhaps because he is bored, needs to relieve tension or just likes to chew. That is why it is important to redirect his chewing when he is still young.

replace your finger with an appropriate chew toy. Your Pekingese does not mean any harm with a friendly nip, but he also does not know how sharp his teeth can be.

CRYING/WHINING

Your pup will often cry, whine, whimper, howl or make some type of commotion when he is left alone. This is basically his way of calling out for attention to make sure that you know he is there and that you have not forgotten about him. He feels insecure when he is left alone, when you are out of the house and he is in his crate or when you are in another part of the house and he cannot see you. The noise he is making is an expression of the anxiety he feels at being alone, so he needs to be taught that being alone is okay. You are not actually training the dog to stop making noise, you are training him to feel comfortable when he is alone and thus removing the need for him to make the noise.

This is where the crate is particularly useful. You want to know that your Peke is safe when you are not there to supervise, and you know that he will be safe in his crate rather than roaming freely about the house. In order for the pup to stay in his crate without making a fuss, he needs to be comfortable in his crate. On that note, it is extremely important that the crate is never used as a form of punishment, or the pup will develop a negative association with the crate.

Accustom the pup to the crate in short, gradually increasing time intervals in which you put him in the crate, maybe with a treat, and stay in the room with him. If he cries or makes a fuss, do not go to him, but stay in his sight. Gradually he will realize that staying in his crate is just fine without your help, and it will not be so traumatic for him when you are not around. You may want to leave the radio on softly when you leave the house; the sound of human voices may be comforting to him.

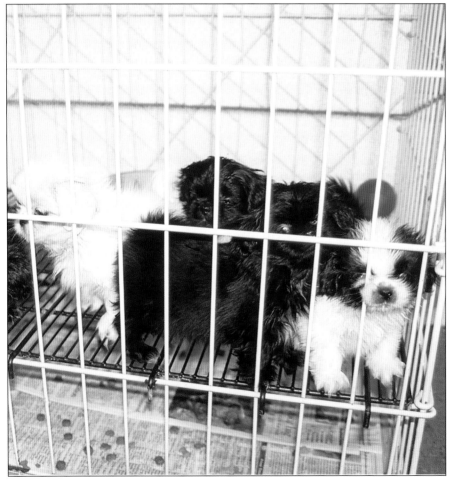

It's advantageous to a new owner if his pup has been introduced to a crate before the pup comes home. This means that the pup is already on his way to accepting the crate as his retreat, which is useful in so many ways.

DIETARY AND FEEDING CONSIDERATIONS

Today the choices of food for your Pekingese are many and varied. There are simply dozens of brands of food in all sorts of flavors and textures, ranging from puppy diets to those for seniors. There are hypoallergenic and low-calorie diets available, and "small bite" foods for small breeds. Because your Pekingese's food has a bearing on coat, health and temperament, it is essential that the most suitable diet be selected for a Pekingese of his age. It is fair to say, however, that even dedicated owners can be somewhat perplexed by the enormous range of foods available. Only under-standing what is best for your dog will help you make an informed decision.

Dog foods are produced in three basic types: dry, semi-moist and canned. Dry foods are useful for the cost-conscious, for overall they tend to be less expensive than semi-moist or canned. These contain the least fat and the most preservatives. In

TIPPING THE SCALES

Good nutrition is vital to your dog's health, but many people end up over-feeding or giving unnecessary supple-ments. Here are some common doggie diet don'ts:

- Adding milk, yogurt and cheese to your dog's diet may seem like a good idea for coat and skin care, but dairy products are very fattening and can cause indigestion.
- Diets high in fat will not cause heart attacks in dogs but will certainly cause your dog to gain weight.
- Most importantly, don't assume your dog will simply stop eating once he doesn't need any more food. Given the chance, he will eat you out of house and home!

general, canned foods are made up of 60–70% water, while semi-moist ones often contain so much sugar that they are perhaps the least preferred by owners, even though their dogs seem to like them.

FEEDING TIPS

- Dog food must be served at room temperature, neither too hot nor too cold. Fresh water, changed often and served in a clean bowl, is mandatory, especially when feeding dry food.
- Never feed your dog from the table while you are eating, and never feed your dog leftovers from your own meal. They usually contain too much fat and too much seasoning.
- Dogs must chew their food. Hard pellets are excellent; soups and stews are to be avoided.
- Don't add leftovers or any extras to commercial dog food. The normal food is usually balanced, and adding something extra destroys the balance.
- Except for age-related changes, dogs do not require dietary variations. They can be fed the same diet, day after day, without their becoming bored or ill.

When selecting your dog's diet, three stages of development must be considered: the puppy stage, the adult stage and the senior stage.

PUPPY STAGE

Puppies instinctively want to suck milk from their mother's teats and a normal puppy will exhibit this behavior from just a few moments following birth. If puppies do not attempt to suckle within the first half-hour or so, the breeder must encourage them to do so by placing them on the nipples, having selected ones with plenty of milk. This early milk supply is important in providing colostrum to protect the puppies during the first eight to ten weeks of their lives.

Although a mother's milk is much better than any milk formula, despite there being some excellent ones available, if the puppies do not feed, they will need to be hand-fed. Puppies should be allowed to nurse from their mothers for about the first six weeks, although, from the third or fourth week, the breeder will begin to introduce small portions of suitable solid food. Most breeders like to introduce alternate milk and meat meals initially, building up to weaning time.

By the time the puppies are seven or a maximum of eight

Breeders start the pups on solid food before they are fully weaned.

Peke puppies should nurse from their mother during the first month of their life, after which the weaning process begins gradually.

weeks old, they should be fully weaned and fed solely on a proprietary puppy food. Selection of the most suitable, good-quality diet at this time is essential, for a puppy's fastest growth rate is during the first year of life. Vets and breeders are able to offer advice in this regard. The frequency of meals will be reduced over time, and eventually the pup will be switched to an adult diet. Puppy and junior diets should be well balanced for the needs of your dog, so that, except in certain circumstances,

CHANGE IN DIET

As your dog's caretaker, you know the importance of keeping his diet consistent, but sometimes when you run out of food or if you're on vacation, you have to make a change quickly. Some dogs will experience digestive problems, but most will not. If you are planning on changing your dog's menu, do so gradually to ensure that your dog will not have any problems. Over a period of four to five days, slowly add some new food to your dog's old food, increasing the percentage of new food each day.

supplementation with additional vitamins, minerals and proteins will not be required.

ADULT DIETS

A dog is considered an adult when he has stopped growing, so in general the diet of a Pekingese will be changed to an adult one by 10 or 12 months of age, or sometimes sooner, depending on the type of food given. There are many specially prepared diets available, but do keep in mind that breeds such as the Pekingese generally do not require a particularly high protein content. This applies especially to those that have been spayed or neutered. It is important that you select the food best suited to your dog's needs, for more active dogs will require a different diet from those leading very sedate lives. Something else to consider is that too much milk, or other dairy products, can sometimes cause upset tummies.

SENIOR DIETS

As dogs get older, their metabolism changes. The older dog usually exercises less, moves more slowly and sleeps more. This change in lifestyle and physiological performance requires a change in diet. Since these changes take place slowly, they might not be recognizable. What is easily recognizable is weight gain. By continuing to feed your dog an adult-maintenance diet when he is slowing down metabolically, your dog will gain weight. Obesity in an older dog compounds the health problems that already accompany old age, and obesity at any age can contribute to back problems.

As your dog gets older, few of his organs function up to par. The kidneys slow down and the intestines become less efficient. These age-related factors are best handled with a change in diet and a change in feeding schedule to give smaller portions that are more easily digested.

STORING DOG FOOD

You must store your dry dog food carefully. Open packages of dog food quickly lose their vitamin value, usually within 90 days of being opened. Mold spores and vermin could also contaminate the food.

There is no single best diet for every older dog. While many dogs do well on light or senior diets, other dogs do better on puppy diets or special premium diets such as lamb and rice. Be sensitive to your senior Pekingese's diet and this will help control other problems that may arise with your old friend.

WATER
Just as your dog needs proper nutrition from his food, water is an essential "nutrient" as well. Water keeps the dog's body properly hydrated and promotes normal function of the body's systems. During housebreaking, it is necessary to keep an eye on how much water your Pekingese is drinking and when, but, once he is reliably trained, he should have access to clean fresh water at all times. Make sure that the dog's water bowl is clean, and change the water often, making

FOOD PREFERENCE
Selecting the best dry dog food is difficult. There is no majority consensus among veterinary scientists as to the value of nutrient analysis (protein, fat, fiber, moisture, ash, cholesterol, minerals, etc.). All agree that feeding trials are what matter most, but you also have to consider the individual dog. The dog's weight, age and activity level, and what pleases his taste, all must be considered. It is probably best to take the advice of your veterinarian. Every dog has individual dietary requirements, and should be fed accordingly.

If your dog is fed a good dry food, he does not require supplements of meat or vegetables. Dogs do appreciate a little variety in their diets, so you may choose to stay with the same brand but vary the flavor. Alternatively, you may wish to add a little flavored stock to give a difference to the taste.

sure that water is always available for your dog, especially if you feed dry food.

EXERCISE
Although a Pekingese is small, all dogs require some form of exercise, regardless of breed. A sedentary lifestyle is as harmful to a dog as it is to a person, but the Pekingese is a not an overly active breed. Regular walks, play sessions in the yard, or letting the dog run free in a fenced area under your supervision are suffi-

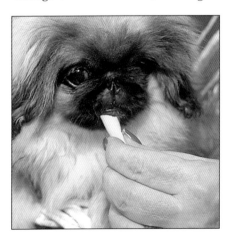

Your Peke will appreciate a treat now and then, but make his snacks healthy ones to avoid contributing to weight gain.

A Worthy Investment

**Veterinary studies have proven that a balanced high-quality diet
pays off in your dog's coat quality, behavior and activity level.
Invest in premium brands for the maximum payoff with your dog.**

Although the Pekingese does not require as much daily exercise as many other breeds, all dogs welcome the opportunity for a walk with a favorite person.

cient forms of exercise for the Pekingese.

Bear in mind that an over-weight dog should never be suddenly over-exercised; instead, he should be allowed to increase exercise slowly. Also remember that not only is exercise essential to keep the dog's body fit, it is essential to his mental well-being. A bored dog will find something to do, which often manifests itself in some type of destructive behavior. In this sense, it is essential for the owner's mental well-being as well!

GROOMING

Your Pekingese will need to be groomed regularly, so it is essential that short grooming sessions be introduced from a very early age. From the very beginning, a few minutes each day should be set aside, the duration building up slowly as the puppy matures and the coat grows in length.

Different breeders use different methods of grooming, and you will eventually find the particular way that suits you and your Peke best. Some groom their dogs on their laps, but most do so on grooming tables. It is important that the table has a non-slip surface. Under no circumstances leave your Pekingese alone on the table, for he may all too easily jump off, which would be dangerous.

DRINK, DRANK, DRUNK— MAKE IT A DOUBLE

In both humans and dogs, as well as other living organisms, water forms the major part of nearly every body tissue. Naturally, we take water for granted, but without it, life as we know it would cease.

For dogs, water is needed to keep their bodies functioning biochemically. Additionally, water is needed to replace the water lost while panting. Unlike humans, who are able to sweat to dissipate heat, dogs must pant to cool down, thereby losing the vital water that their bodies need to regulate their body temperatures. Humans lose electrolyte-containing products and other body-fluid components through sweating; dogs do not lose anything except water.

Water is essential always, but especially so when the weather is hot or humid or when your dog is exercising or working vigorously.

GETTING STARTED

When the puppy is used to standing on the table, you will probably find it useful to teach him to be rolled over onto his back. You will do this by putting your hand under the puppy's back, with your fingers pointing toward his head. The other hand will be used underneath for support. Turn the puppy gently over and hold him there reassuringly, speaking to him all the while and stroking him. At this early stage, do not attempt to do anything that would hurt the puppy, for he will need to accept this as a pleasurable experience. You must always be sure to have one hand firmly in control in case the puppy wriggles. In the event of his wriggling and turning back again, just repeat the exercise, always remembering that it is you who must have the

It will be much easier to begin grooming the puppy—and the puppy coat. As your Peke grows up and his coat grows longers, grooming will become a more involved task, and you want your dog to be comfortable with it.

"DOES THIS COLLAR MAKE ME LOOK FAT?"

While humans may obsess about how they look and how trim their bodies are, many people believe that extra weight on their dogs is a good thing. The truth is, pets should not be over- or underweight, as both can lead to or signal sickness. In order to tell how fit your pet is, run your hands over his ribs. Are his ribs buried under a layer of fat or are they sticking out considerably? If your pet is within his normal weight range, you should be able to feel the ribs easily, but they should not protrude abnormally. If you stand above him, the outline of his body should resemble an hourglass. Some breeds do tend to be leaner while some are a bit stockier, like the Peke, but making sure your dog is the right weight for his breed will certainly contribute to his good health.

upper hand. Be firm, but always kind.

When you know he is comfortable with this, introduce a few gentle brush strokes with your pin brush. This may take a little getting used to both for you and your puppy. If your Peke learns to roll over, you will more easily be able to groom in all the awkward places, such as under the "armpits," in the groin area, under the chin and behind the ears. You will both be glad you had a little patience in learning this trick from the very start!

ROUTINE GROOMING

To keep your Peke looking in tip-top condition, it is important to keep the coat clean and to groom regularly, though owners of Pekingese do not generally bathe their dogs as frequently as do owners of other long-coated breeds. It is a good idea to set aside ten minutes or so each day, for a neglected coat not only will look unpleasant but also will be uncomfortable for your dog. All grooming equipment must be kept clean and in good condition.

Never groom a coat when completely dry, but use a fine water spray, light coat dressing, or even a mixture of conditioner and water (about one tablespoon of conditioner to half a cup of water). This will help avoid the removal of too much coat and

FREE AT LAST!

While walking off-leash may be great fun for your dog, it can turn into a time when your dog shows you everything you did wrong in obedience class. If you want to give your dog a chance to have some fun and exercise without the constraints of a leash, a good place to do this is in a designated fenced-in area where dogs can socialize and work off excess energy. When visiting such an area, don't let your dog run amok or unattended, watch other dogs that are present and follow all rules, specifically those regarding waste disposal.

---

will prevent hair breakage.

Doubtless you will pick up some grooming tips from other Pekingese enthusiasts if you visit shows, and in time you will decide upon the method that works best for you. Whether grooming on a table or, if you prefer, on your lap, you must work methodically through the coat. Spray each section of the coat and work through it layer by layer with your pin brush, grooming right down to the skin. Many people like to start under the chin and work backward to the hindquarters.

A snooping Peke invites all kinds of things to get caught in his coat—always pay special attention to checking the coat when he returns from outdoor expeditions.

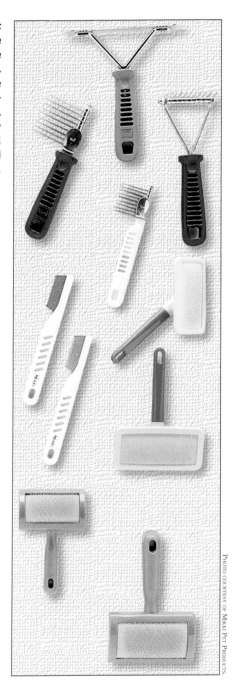

PHOTO COURTESY OF MIKKI PET PRODUCTS.

When most of the coat has been brushed with the dog lying down, you should stand your dog on the table so that you can brush through the tail feathering, "trousers," forelegs and foot fringes. You will also pay attention to the ear fringing, making certain that no knots have formed behind the ears. These cannot easily be seen, but they certainly can be felt!

It is also important that the corners of the eyes and the wrinkle over the nose are gently cleaned using a moist tissue or cotton ball, then dried with a clean tissue. Some owners like to dry the area above the nose, at the stop, with powder, but of course this must be removed prior to exhibition in the show ring.

GROOMING EQUIPMENT

How much grooming equipment you purchase will depend on how much grooming you are going to do. Here are some basics:

- Pin brush
- Metal comb
- Scissors
- Rubber mat
- Dog shampoo
- Spray hose attachment
- Towels
- Blow dryer
- Ear cleaner
- Cotton balls
- Nail clippers
- Dental care products

FINISHING OFF

The finishing touches on the coat are done in such a way to emphasize the characteristics of the breed, some using just the pin brush, others a wide-toothed comb. The body hair behind the mane is brushed back and down toward the tail, while chest hair is fluffed outward and upward to emphasize the width of the ribs. The mane itself is brushed forward to form a frame around the head. On the top of skull, the hair is brushed flat, emphasizing both width and flatness of the skull. Brushing down the ear fringes to their full length, and finally fluffing them forward, serve to frame the face. For best effect, the bib is brushed down and is then flicked up, another means of giving emphasis to the width of chest.

On the legs, the trousers are brushed downward, and then out, making them look both long and full. The tail has to be brushed on both sides, then laid over the back and brushed forward so that the plume falls over the back and along the side of the body.

BATHING AND DRYING

Companion Pekes really only need bathing when they are dirty, and even show dogs are bathed infrequently. This is because bathing has a tendency to soften the coat, and a soft coat is not required in this breed. If yours is a show dog, on occasions when bathing is needed, it should be done at least a week before the show. It is important that the coat is brushed so that it is free of mats and tangles prior to bathing, for the water will only serve to tighten them.

As with grooming, every owner has his or her own preference as to how best to bathe. I

After your Peke's bath or if his coat gets wet outdoors, keep him wrapped in an absorbent towel to soak up excess water before finishing the job with a blow dryer.

First, thoroughly soak your Peke's coat.

BATHING BEAUTY

Once you are sure that the dog is thoroughly rinsed, squeeze the excess water out of his coat with your hand and dry him with an heavy towel. You may choose to use a blow dryer on his coat or just let it dry naturally. In cold weather, never allow your dog outside with a wet coat.

There are "dry bath" products on the market, which are sprays and powders intended for spot cleaning, that can be used between regular baths if necessary. They are not substitutes for regular baths, but they are easy to use for touch-ups as they do not require rinsing.

Next, apply a special dog shampoo.

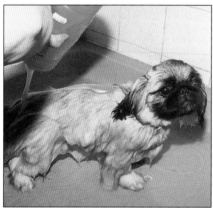

Lather the shampoo thoroughly into the dog's coat.

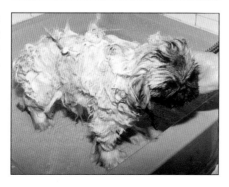

like to stand my own dogs on a non-slip mat in the bath, then wet the coat thoroughly using a shower spray. It is imperative that the water temperature is first tested on your own hand to make sure that the water is neither too hot nor too cold. You should use a good-quality shampoo designed especially for dogs; never use a human-hair product. Always stroke the shampoo into the coat rather than rub, so as not to create knots, and take care not to get soap into the dog's eyes. Some like to plug the ears with cotton to avoid water getting inside them, but personally I have never done this. I have found that just by being extra careful, I have never encountered problems. Finally, lift your dog

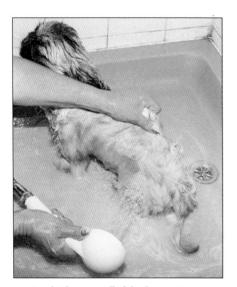

Completely remove all of the shampoo in your Peke's coat.

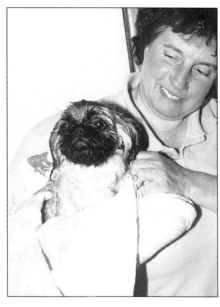

Dry the dog as completely as possible with a soft, clean, dry towel.

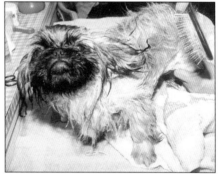

Use a brush and a hair dryer on a low heat setting to complete the drying job.

Your Peke's eyes must be protected at all times. Soap can irritate your Peke's eyes, so take special care during bathing.

carefully out of the bath, wrapped in a warm, clean towel. Undoubtedly your dog will want to shake—so be prepared!

Drying can be done on the same table that you use for the grooming process, or even on your lap. Work systematically, applying warm (not hot!) air from the blow dryer, concentrating on one area at a time.

The head is usually left until last. For this, the best method usually seems to be for your dog to be in a sitting position. Many dogs do not like warm air blowing directly toward their eyes and noses, so take this into consideration when angling the blow dryer.

After a good bath and thorough drying, your Peke can be given the final touches.

TRIMMING

Feet should always be checked thoroughly for any dirt trapped between the pads and for knots that may have formed. The hair that grows between the pads should be scissored carefully, as any build-up of knots or debris causes discomfort and can disturb movement.

EAR CLEANING

The Pekingese's hair will also grow inside the ears. This should be carefully plucked out with blunt-ended tweezers. Remove only a few hairs at a time and this should be entirely painless.

NAIL FILING

You can purchase an electric tool to grind down a dog's nails rather than cut them. Some dogs don't seem to mind the electric grinder but will object strongly to nail clippers. Talking it over with your veterinarian will help you make the right choice.

Ears must always be kept clean. This can be done using a special liquid cleaner with cotton wool or cotton balls. Many people use cotton swabs, but extreme care must be taken not to delve too deeply into the ears, as this can cause injury. Be on the lookout for any signs of infection or ear-mite infestation. If your Pekingese has been shaking his head or scratching at his ears frequently, this usually indicates a problem. If his ears have an unusual odor, this is a sure sign of mite infestation or infection, and a signal to have his ears checked by the vet.

NAIL CLIPPING

Your Pekingese should be accustomed to having his nails trimmed at an early age, since it will be part of your maintenance routine throughout his life. Long nails are uncomfortable for any dog and can be sharp if they scratch someone unintentionally. Also, a long nail has a better chance of ripping and bleeding, or causing the feet to spread. A good rule of thumb is that if you can hear your dog's nails' clicking on the floor when he walks,

his nails are too long.

Before you start cutting, make sure you can identify the "quick" in each nail. The quick is a blood vessel that runs through the center of each nail and grows rather close to the end. It will bleed if accidentally cut, which will be quite painful for the dog as it contains nerve endings. Keep some type of clot-

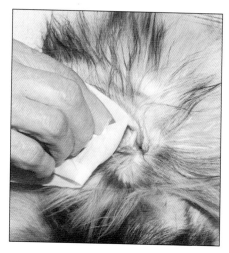

Clean the outer ear gently with a soft wipe, never delving into the ear canal or probing where your cannot see.

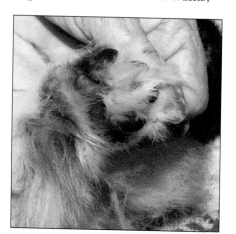

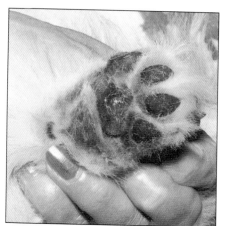

Left: The foot before trimming. Right: The foot after trimming, looking neat and tidy.

Your Peke's nails should be clipped on a regular basis with a nail clipper made for use on dogs.

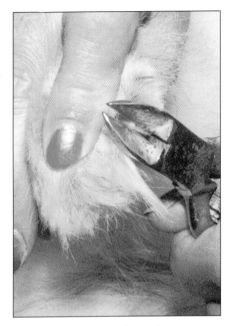

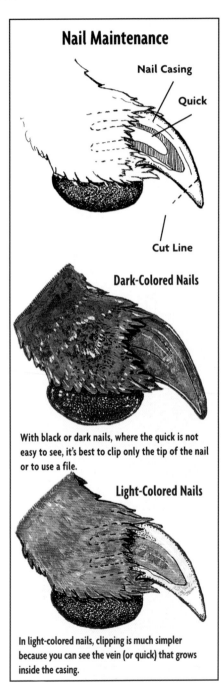

Nail Maintenance

Nail Casing

Quick

Cut Line

Dark-Colored Nails

With black or dark nails, where the quick is not easy to see, it's best to clip only the tip of the nail or to use a file.

Light-Colored Nails

In light-colored nails, clipping is much simpler because you can see the vein (or quick) that grows inside the casing.

ting agent on hand, such as a styptic pencil or styptic powder (the type used for shaving). This will stop the bleeding quickly when applied to the end of the cut nail. Do not panic if you cut the quick, just stop the bleeding and talk soothingly to your dog. Once he has calmed down, move on to the next nail. It is better to clip a little at a time, particularly when the quick is not visable.

Hold your pup steady as you begin trimming his nails; you do not want him to make any sudden movements or run away. Talk to him soothingly and stroke him as you clip. Holding his foot in your hand, simply take off the end of each nail in one quick clip. You can purchase nail clip-

On the grooming table before his turn in the ring, this Peke gets a pre-show grooming to ensure that he looks his best for the judge.

MOTION SICKNESS

*If life is a motorway...*your dog may not want to come along for the ride! Some dogs experience motion sickness in cars that leads to excessive salivation and even vomiting. In most cases, your dog will fare better in the familiar, safe confines of his crate. To desensitize your dog, try going on several short jaunts before trying a long trip. If your dog experiences distress when riding in the vehicle, drive with him only when absolutely necessary, and do not feed him or give him water before you go.

pers that are specially made for dogs; you can probably find them wherever you buy pet or grooming supplies.

If your Peke still has his dewclaws intact, don't forget to trim them short, as they are very prone to getting caught on blankets, furniture or bushes.

TRAVELING WITH YOUR DOG

CAR TRAVEL

You should accustom your Pekingese to riding in a car at an early age. You may or may not take him in the car often, but at the very least he will need to go to the vet and you do not want these trips to be traumatic for the dog or troublesome for you. The safest way for a dog to ride in the car is in his crate. If he uses a crate in the house, you can use the same crate for travel. Put the pup in the crate and see how he reacts. If the puppy seems uneasy, you can have a passenger hold him on his lap while you drive. Do not let the dog roam loose in the vehicle—this is very dangerous! If you should stop short, your dog can be thrown and injured. If the dog starts climbing on you and pestering you while you are driving, you will not be able to concentrate on the road. It is an unsafe situation for everyone—human and canine.

For long trips, be prepared to stop to let the dog relieve himself. Bring along whatever you need to clean up after him. You should take along some paper towels and perhaps some old rags or bath towels for use should he have a potty accident in the car or suffer from motion sickness.

AIR TRAVEL

Contact your chosen airline before proceeding with your travel plans that include your Pekingese, as extra precautions must be taken when flying with a brachycephalic breed. The dog will be required to travel in a fiberglass crate, and brachycephalic breeds must travel in a crate that is one size larger than normal, and with extra ventilation. You also must include water in your Peke's crate and make sure that he is well accustomed to the travel crate. This can be done by letting him spend time in the travel crate, instead of his usual crate, for several days before the trip. You should always check in advance with the airline regarding any other specific crate requirements, as the crate must be airline-approved.

On many airlines, small pets whose crates fall within the specified size limitations are granted "carry-on" status and can accompany their owners in the cabin in their crates. This may be possible

TRAVELING ABROAD

For international travel, you will have to make arrangements well in advance (perhaps months), as countries' regulations pertaining to bringing in animals differ. There may be special health certificates and/or vaccinations that your dog will need before taking the trip; sometimes this has to be done within a certain time frame. In rabies-free countries, you will need to bring proof of the dog's rabies vaccination and there may be a quarantine period upon arrival.

Although your Peke may try to convince you that he should take the wheel, he should never travel in a car without being properly secured either in a crate or with a special car harness.

Ex-pens are easily portable to bring along when you travel and give your Peke a secure place to stretch his legs wherever you go.

with your Peke; check with various airlines before booking your flight to see which ones will give your Peke "first-class" treatment.

To help put the dog at ease for the trip, give him one of his favorite toys in the crate. Do not feed the dog for several hours prior to checking in so that you minimize his need to relieve himself. Some airlines require you to provide documentation as to when the dog has last been fed. In any case, a light meal is best. If your Peke is not able to travel in the cabin with you, you will have to attach food and water bowls to the outside of the dog's crate so that airline employees can tend to him between legs of the trip.

Make sure your that your Peke is properly identified and that your contact information appears on his ID tags and on his crate. If not permitted in the cabin, your Pekingese will travel in a different area of the plane than the human passengers, so every rule must be strictly followed to prevent the slight risk of getting separated from your dog. Keep in mind, though, that transporting pets is rather routine for large carriers.

VACATIONS AND BOARDING

So you want to take a family vacation—and you want to include *all* members of the family. You would probably make arrangements for accommodation ahead of time anyway, but this is especially important when traveling with a dog. You do not want to make an overnight stop at the only place around for miles and find out that they do not allow dogs. Also, you do not want to reserve a place for your family without confirming that you are traveling with a dog because, if it is against their policy, you may not have a place to stay.

Alternatively, if you are travel-

Show dogs travel more than other dogs, being constantly toted about every weekend for exhibition. These competitive Pekes are the "frequent flyers" (or drivers) of the dog world. This is the Pekingese booth at the Crufts Dog Show, the UK's largest show.

ing and choose not to bring your Pekingese, you will have to make arrangements for him while you are away. Some options are to take him to a friend's house to stay while you are gone, to have a trusted friend stop by often or stay at your house or to bring your dog to a reputable boarding kennel. If you choose to board him at a kennel, you should visit in advance to see the facilities provided, how clean they are and where the dogs are kept. Talk to some of the employees and see how they treat the dogs. Learn if they have experience in groom-

> **TRAVEL TIP**
> Never leave *any* dog alone in the car. In hot weather, your dog can die from the high temperature inside a closed vehicle; even a car parked in the shade can heat up very quickly. Leaving the window open is dangerous as well since the dog can hurt himself trying to get out. Pekes are especially heat-sensitive.

ing long-coated dogs, if they spend time with the dogs, play with them, exercise them, etc.? Also find out the kennel's policy on vaccinations and what they require. This is for all of the

Seek out a boarding facility that can care for Toy dogs properly. Do your research and visit the kennel before you actually need to use it so that you can feel more comfortable with leaving your Peke while you are on vacation.

dogs' safety, since when dogs are kept together, there is a greater risk of diseases being passed from dog to dog.

IDENTIFICATION

Your Pekingese is your valued companion and friend. That is why you always keep a close eye on him and you have made sure that he cannot escape from the yard or wriggle out of his collar and run away from you. However, accidents can happen and there may come a time when your dog unexpectedly gets separated from you. If this unfortunate event should occur, the first thing on your mind will be finding him. Proper identification, including an ID tag, and possibly a tattoo and/or a microchip, will increase the chances of his being returned to you safely and quickly.

IDENTIFICATION OPTIONS

As puppies become more and more expensive, especially those puppies of high quality for showing and/or breeding, they have a greater chance of being stolen. The usual collar dog tag is, of course, easily removed. But there are two more permanent techniques that have become widely used for identification purposes.

The puppy microchip implantation involves the injection of a small microchip, about the size of a corn kernel, under the skin of the dog. If your dog shows up at a clinic or shelter, or is offered for resale under less-than-savory circumstances, he can be positively identified by the microchip. The microchip is scanned, and a registry quickly identifies you as the owner.

Tattooing is done on various parts of the dog, from his belly to his ears. The number tattooed can be your telephone number, your dog's registration number or any other number that you can easily memorize. When professional dog thieves see a tattooed dog, they usually lose interest. For the safety of our dogs, no laboratory facility or dog broker will accept a tattooed dog as stock.

Discuss microchipping and tattooing with your vet and breeder. Some vets perform these services on their own premises for a reasonable fee. To ensure the effectiveness of your dog's ID, be certain that the dog is then properly registered with a legitimate national database.

Every dog should always have proper identification tags attached to his everyday collar.

TRAINING YOUR
PEKINGESE

Living with an untrained dog is a lot like owning a piano that you do not know how to play—it is a nice object to look at, but it does not do much more than that to bring you pleasure. Now try taking piano lessons, and suddenly the piano comes alive and brings forth magical sounds and rhythms that set your heart singing and your body swaying.

The same is true with your Pekingese. Any dog is a big responsibility and, if not trained sensibly, may develop unacceptable behavior that annoys you or could even cause family friction.

To train your Pekingese, you may like to enroll in an obedience class. Teach him good manners as you learn how and why he behaves the way he does. Find out how to communicate with your dog and how to recognize and understand his communications with you. Suddenly the dog takes on a new role in your life—he is clever, interesting, well-behaved and fun to be with. He demonstrates his bond of devotion to you daily. In other words, your

Pekingese does wonders for your ego because he constantly reminds you that you are not only his leader, you are his hero!

Those involved with teaching dog obedience and counseling owners about their dogs' behavior have discovered some interesting facts about dog ownership. For example, training dogs when they are puppies results in the highest rate of success in developing well-mannered and well-adjusted adult dogs. Training an older dog, from six months to six years of age, can produce almost equal results, providing that the owner accepts the dog's slower rate of learning capability and is willing to work patiently to help the dog succeed at developing to his fullest potential. Unfortunately, many owners of untrained adult dogs lack the patience factor, so they do not persist until their dogs are successful at learning particular behaviors.

Training a puppy, aged 10 to 16 weeks (20 weeks at the most), is like working with a dry sponge in a pool of water. The pup soaks up whatever you show him and constantly looks for more things to do and learn. At this early age, his body is not yet producing hormones, and therein lies the reason for such a high rate of success. Without hormones, he is focused on his owners and not particularly interested in investigating other places, dogs, people, etc. You are his leader: his provider of food, water, shelter and security. He latches onto you and wants to stay close. He will usually follow you from room to room,

REAP THE REWARDS

If you start with a normal, healthy dog and give him time, patience and some carefully executed lessons, you will reap the rewards of that training for the life of the dog. And what a life it will be! The two of you will find immeasurable pleasure in the companionship you have built together with love, respect and understanding.

will not let you out of his sight when you are outdoors with him and will respond in like manner to the people and animals you encounter. If you greet a friend warmly, he will be happy to greet the person as well. If, however, you are hesitant or anxious about the approach of a stranger, he will respond accordingly.

Pekes don't need special training to do their signature "dance." Produce a treat and watch your Peke spring into action!

THINK BEFORE YOU BARK

Dogs are sensitive to their masters' moods and emotions. Use your voice wisely when communicating with your dog. Never raise your voice at your dog unless you are trying to correct him. "Barking" at your dog can become as meaningless as "dogspeak" is to you.

Once the puppy begins to produce hormones, his natural curiosity emerges and he begins to investigate the world around him. It is at this time when you may notice that the untrained dog begins to wander away from you and even ignore your commands to stay close.

There usually will be classes within a reasonable distance of your home, but you can also do a lot to train your dog yourself. Sometimes there are classes available, but the tuition is too costly. Whatever the circumstances, the solution to training your Pekingese without formal obedience lessons lies within the pages of this book. This chapter is devoted to helping you train your Pekingese at home. If the recommended procedures are followed faithfully, you may expect positive results that will prove rewarding to both you and your dog.

Whether your new charge is a puppy or a mature adult, the methods of teaching and the techniques we use in training basic behaviors are the same. After all, no dog, whether puppy or adult, likes harsh or inhumane methods. All creatures, however, respond favorably to gentle motivational methods and sincere praise and encouragement. Now let us get started.

HOUSEBREAKING

You can train a puppy to relieve himself wherever you choose, but this must be somewhere suitable. You should bear in mind from the outset that when your puppy is old enough to go out in public places, any canine droppings must be removed at once. You will always have to carry with you a small plastic bag or "poop-scoop."

Outdoor training includes such surfaces as grass, soil and cement. Indoor training usually means training your dog to newspaper. When deciding on the surface and location that you will want your Pekingese to use, be sure it is going to be permanent. Training your dog to grass and then changing your mind two months later is extremely difficult for both dog and owner.

Next, choose the command you will use each and every time you want your puppy to relieve himself. "Let's go," "Hurry up" and "Potty" are examples of commands

CALM DOWN

Dogs will do anything for your attention. If you reward the dog when he is calm and attentive, you will develop a well-mannered dog. If, on the other hand, you greet your dog excitedly and encourage him to wrestle with you, the dog will greet you the same way and you will have a hyperactive dog on your hands.

Teaching the house rules is an integral part of your Peke's training. Will he be allowed on the furniture? If so, that's fine; if not, be consistent in not letting him lounge on the sofa.

Don't let your Peke roam in the flowerbeds. Pick your Peke's relief spot in an out-of-the-way part of the yard and train him always to use the same place.

PAPER CAPER

Never line your pup's sleeping area with newspaper. Puppy litters are usually raised on newspaper and, once in your home, the puppy will immediately associate newspaper with voiding. Never put newspaper on any floor while housebreaking, as this will only confuse the puppy. If you are paper-training him, use paper in his designated relief area only. Finally, restrict water intake after evening meals. Offer a few licks at a time—never let a young puppy gulp water after meals.

commonly used by dog owners.

Get in the habit of giving the puppy your chosen relief command before you take him out. That way, when he becomes an adult, you will be able to determine if he wants to go out when you ask him. A confirmation will be signs of interest, such as wagging his tail, watching you intently, going to the door, etc.

PUPPY'S NEEDS

Puppy needs to relieve himself after play periods, after each

CANINE DEVELOPMENT SCHEDULE

It is important to understand how and at what age a puppy develops into adulthood.
If you are a puppy owner, consult the following Canine Development Schedule to
determine the stage of development your puppy is currently experiencing.
This knowledge will help you as you work with the puppy in the weeks and months ahead.

Period	Age	Characteristics
First to Third	**Birth to Seven Weeks**	Puppy needs food, sleep and warmth, and responds to simple and gentle touching. Needs mother for security and disciplining. Needs littermates for learning and interacting with other dogs. Pup learns to function within a pack and learns pack order of dominance. Begin socializing pup with adults and children for short periods. Pup begins to become aware of his environment.
Fourth	**Eight to Twelve Weeks**	Brain is fully developed. Needs socializing with outside world. Remove from mother and littermates. Needs to change from canine pack to human pack. Human dominance necessary. Fear period occurs between 8 and 12 weeks. Avoid fright and pain.
Fifth	**Thirteen to Sixteen Weeks**	Training and formal obedience should begin. Less association with other dogs, more with people, places, situations. Period will pass easily if you remember this is pup's change-to-adolescence time. Be firm and fair. Flight instinct prominent. Permissiveness and over-disciplining can do permanent damage. Praise for good behavior.
Juvenile	**Four to Eight Months**	Another fear period about 7 to 8 months of age. It passes quickly, but be cautious of fright and pain. Sexual maturity reached. Dominant traits established. Dog should understand sit, down, come and stay by now.

Note: These are approximate time frames. Allow for individual differences in puppies.

Pekes, as do most other dogs, like a den-like place to call their own. A soft bed under a chair is this Peke's favorite spot.

meal, after he has been sleeping and any time he indicates that he is looking for a place to urinate or defecate. The urinary and intestinal tract muscles of very young puppies are not fully developed. Therefore, like human babies, puppies need to relieve themselves frequently.

Take your puppy out often—every hour for a 12-week-old, for example, and always immediately after sleeping and eating. The older the puppy, the more control he will have and the less often he will need to relieve himself. Finally, as a mature healthy adult, he will require only three to five relief trips per day.

HOUSING

Since the type of housing and control you provide for your puppy have a direct relationship on the success of housebreaking, we consider the various aspects

of both before we begin training.

Bringing a new puppy home and turning him loose in your house can be compared to turning a child loose in an amusement park and telling the child that the place is all his! The sheer enormity of the place would be too much for him to handle.

Instead, offer the puppy clearly defined areas where he can play, sleep, eat and live. A room of the house where the family gathers is the most obvious choice. Puppies are social animals and need to feel a part of the pack right from the start. Hearing your voice, watching you while you are doing things and smelling you nearby are all positive reinforcers that he is now a member of your pack. Usually a family room, the kitchen or a nearby adjoining breakfast area is ideal for providing safety and security for

---

THE GOLDEN RULE

The golden rule of dog training is simple. For each "question" (command), there is only one correct answer (reaction). One command = one reaction. Keep practicing the command until the dog reacts correctly without hesitating. Be repetitive but not monotonous. Dogs get bored just as people do!

both puppy and owner.

Within that room, there should be a smaller area that the puppy can call his own. An alcove, a wire or fiberglass dog crate or a partitioned (not boarded!) corner from which he can view the activities of his new family will be fine. The size of the area or crate is the key factor here. The area must be large enough for the puppy to lie down and stretch out as well as stand up without rubbing his head on the top, yet small enough so that he cannot relieve himself at one end and sleep at the other without coming into contact with his droppings during the housebreaking process. Dogs are, by nature, clean animals and will not remain close to their relief areas unless forced to do so. In those cases, they then become dirty dogs and usually remain that way for life.

The designated area should contain clean bedding and a toy. Water must always be available, in a non-spill container, although you should avoid putting food and water in the dog's crate until he is reliably housebroken.

CONTROL
By control, we mean helping the puppy to create a lifestyle pattern that will be compatible to that of his human pack *(you!)*.

Just as we guide little children to learn our way of life, we must show the puppy when it is time to play, eat, sleep, exercise and even entertain himself.

Your puppy should always sleep in his crate. He should also learn that, during times of household confusion and excessive human activity, such as at breakfast when family members are preparing for the day, he can

COMMAND STANCE
Stand up straight and authoritatively when giving your dog commands. Do not issue commands when lying on the floor or lying on your back on the sofa. If you are on your hands and knees when you give a command, your dog will think you are positioning yourself to play.

Wire crates are popular for use in the home because they keep the dog secure while allowing him to see all around him and feel a part of his surroundings.

play by himself in relative safety and comfort in his designated area. Each time you leave the puppy alone, he should understand exactly where he is to stay. You can gradually increase the time he is left alone to get him used to it.

Puppies are chewers. They cannot tell the difference between things like lamp cords, television wires, shoes, table legs, etc. Chewing into a television wire, for example, can be fatal to the puppy, while a shorted wire can start a fire in the house.

If the puppy chews on the arm of the chair when he is alone, you will probably discipline him angrily when you get home. Thus, he makes the association that your coming home means he is going to be punished. (He will not remember chewing the chair and is incapable of making the association of the discipline with his naughty deed.) Keeping the pup crated when you're not there to

Train yourself to clean up every time your dog relieves himself, even if it's in your own yard.

supervise keeps him from engaging in destructive and or dangerous behaviors.

Times of excitement, such as family parties, friends' visits, etc., can be fun for the puppy, providing he can view the activities from the security of his designated area. He is not underfoot and he is not being fed all sorts of tidbits that will

probably cause him stomach distress, yet he still feels a part of the fun.

SCHEDULE

A puppy should be taken to his relief area each time he is released from his designated area, after meals, after play sessions and when he first awakens in the morning (at age 12 weeks, this can mean 5 a.m.!). The puppy will indicate that he's ready "to go" by circling or sniffing busily—do not misinterpret these signs. When you first bring your puppy home, a routine of taking him out every hour is necessary. As the puppy grows, he will be able to wait for longer periods of time.

Keep trips to his relief area short. Stay no more than five or six minutes and then return to the house. If he goes during that time, praise him lavishly and take him indoors immediately. If he does not, but he has an accident when you go back indoors, pick him up immediately, say

"No! No!" and return to his relief area. Wait a few minutes, then return to the house again. Never hit a puppy or put his face in urine or excrement when he has had an accident!

Once indoors, put the puppy in his crate until you have had time to clean up his accident. Then release him to the family area and watch him more closely than before. Chances are, his accident was a result of your not picking up his signal or waiting too long before offering him the opportunity to relieve himself. Never hold a grudge against the puppy for accidents.

Let the puppy learn that going outdoors means it is time to relieve himself, not to play. Once trained, he will be able to play indoors and out and still differentiate between the times

Keeping your Peke puppy occupied with safe toys keeps his mind off making mischief.

TAKE THE LEAD

Do not carry your dog to his relief area. Lead him there on a leash or, better yet, encourage him to follow you to the spot. If you start carrying him to his spot, you might end up doing this routine forever and your dog will have the satisfaction of having trained *you.*

for play versus the times for relieving himself.

Help him develop regular hours for naps, being alone, playing by himself and just resting, all in his crate. Encourage him to entertain himself while you are busy with your activities. Let him learn that having

you near is comforting, but it is not your main purpose in life to provide him with your undivided attention.

Each time you put your puppy in his own area, use the same command, whatever suits best. Soon, he will run to his crate or special area when he

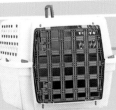

THE SUCCESS METHOD

Success that comes by luck is usually short-lived. Success that comes by well-thought-out proven methods is often more easily achieved and permanent. This is the Success Method. It is designed to give you, the puppy owner, a simple yet proven way to help your puppy develop clean living habits and a feeling of security in his new environment.

6 Steps to Successful Crate Training

1 Tell the puppy "Crate time!" and place him in the crate with a small treat (a piece of cheese or half of a biscuit). Let him stay in the crate for five minutes while you are in the same room. Then release him and praise lavishly. Never release him when he is fussing. Wait until he is quiet before you let him out.

2 Repeat Step 1 several times a day.

3 The next day, place the puppy in the crate as before. Let him stay there for ten minutes. Do this several times.

4 Continue building time in five-minute increments until the puppy stays in his crate for 30 minutes with you in the room. Always take him to his relief area after prolonged periods in his crate.

5 Now go back to Step 1 and let the puppy stay in his crate for five minutes, this time while you are out of the room.

6 Once again, build crate time in five-minute increments with you out of the room. When the puppy will stay willingly in his crate (he may even fall asleep!) for 30 minutes with you out of the room, he will be ready to stay in it for several hours at a time.

HOW MANY TIMES A DAY?

AGE	RELIEF TRIPS
To 14 weeks	10
14–22 weeks	8
22–32 weeks	6
Adulthood	4
(dog stops growing)	

These are estimates, of course, but they are a guide to the *minimum* number of opportunities a dog should have each day to relieve himself.

hears you say those words.

Crate training provides safety for you, the puppy and the home. It also provides the puppy with a feeling of security, and that helps the puppy achieve self-confidence and clean habits. Remember that one of the primary ingredients in housebreaking your puppy is control. Regardless of your lifestyle, there will always be occasions when you will need to have a place where your dog can stay and be happy and safe. Crate training is the answer for now and in the future.

In conclusion, a few key elements are really all you need for a successful housebreaking method—consistency, frequency, praise, control and supervision. By following these procedures with a normal, healthy puppy, you and the puppy will soon be past the stage of "accidents" and ready to move on to a clean and rewarding life together.

ROLES OF DISCIPLINE, REWARD AND PUNISHMENT

Discipline, training one to act in accordance with rules, brings order to life. It is as simple as that. Without discipline, particularly in a group society, chaos reigns supreme and the group will eventually perish. Humans and canines are social animals and need some form of discipline in order to function effectively. They must procure food, reproduce to keep the species going and protect their home base and their young.

If there were no discipline in the lives of social animals, they would eventually die from starvation and/or predation by other stronger animals. In the case of domestic canines, dogs need

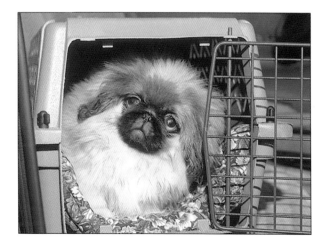

A Peke will welcome time in his crate once he has been acclimated to using it.

TRAINING RULES
If you want to be successful in training your dog, you have four rules to obey yourself:
1. Develop an understanding of how a dog thinks.
2. Do not blame the dog for lack of communication.
3. Define your dog's personality and act accordingly.
4. Have patience and be consistent.

discipline in their lives in order to understand how their pack (you and other family members) functions and how they must act in order to survive.

A large humane society in a highly populated area recently surveyed dog owners regarding their satisfaction with their relationships with their dogs. People who had trained their dogs were 75% more satisfied with their pets than those who had never trained their dogs.

Dr. Edward Thorndike, a noted psychologist, established *Thorndike's Theory of Learning*, which states that a behavior that results in an pleasant event tends to be repeated. A behavior that results in an unpleasant event tends not to be repeated. It is this theory on which training methods are based today. For example, if you manipulate a dog to perform a specific behavior and reward him for doing it,

Have a suitable crate before you bring the pup home. You'll need it right away, as you want him to become adjusted to the crate as he settles into his new home.

he is likely to do it again because he enjoyed the end result.

Occasionally, punishment, a penalty inflicted for an offense, is necessary. The best type of punishment often comes from an outside source. For example, a child is told not to touch the stove because he may get burned. He disobeys and touches the stove. In doing so, he receives a burn. From that time on, he respects the heat of the stove and avoids contact with it. Therefore, a behavior that results in an unpleasant event tends not to be repeated.

A good example of a dog's

learning the hard way is the dog who chases the house cat. He is told many times to leave the cat alone, yet he persists in teasing the cat. Then, one day he begins chasing the cat but the cat turns and swipes a claw across the dog's face, leaving him with a painful gash on his nose. The final result is that the dog stops chasing the cat.

TRAINING EQUIPMENT

COLLAR AND LEASH
For a Pekingese, the collar and leash that you use for training must be one with which you are easily able to work, not too heavy for the dog and perfectly safe.

TREATS
Have a bag of treats on hand. Something nutritious and easy to swallow works best. Use a

The first step in training is to be sure that your Peke's attention is on *you* before you proceed with the lesson.

PLAN TO PLAY
The puppy should also have regular play and exercise sessions when he is with you or a family member. Exercise for a very young puppy can consist of a short walk around the house or yard. Playing can include fetching games with a special toy. (All puppies teethe and need soft things upon which to chew.) Remember to restrict play periods to indoors within his living area (the family room, for example) until he is completely housebroken.

---

soft treat, a chunk of cheese or a piece of cooked chicken rather than a dry biscuit. By the time the dog has finished chewing a dry treat, he will forget why he is being rewarded in the first place! Incidentally, using food rewards will not teach a dog to beg at the table—the only way to teach a dog to beg at the table is to give him food from the table. In training, rewarding the dog with a food treat will help him associate praise and the treats with learning new behaviors that obviously please his owner.

TRAINING BEGINS: ASK THE DOG A QUESTION

In order to teach your dog anything, you must first get his attention. After all, he cannot learn anything if he is looking away from you with his mind on something else.

To get his attention, ask him, "School?" and immediately walk over to him and give him a treat as you tell him "Good dog." Wait a minute or two and repeat the routine, this time with a treat in your hand as you approach within a foot of the dog. Do not go directly to him, but stop about a foot short of him and hold out the treat as you ask, "School?" He will see you approaching with a treat in your hand and most likely begin walking toward you. As you meet, give him the treat and praise again.

The third time, ask the question, have a treat in your hand and walk only a short distance toward the dog so that he must walk almost all the way to you. As he reaches you, give him the treat and praise again.

By this time, the dog will probably be getting the idea that if he pays attention to you, especially when you ask that question, it will pay off in treats and fun activities for him. In other words, he learns that "school" means doing fun things with you that result in treats and positive attention for him.

Remember that the dog does not understand your verbal language, he only recognizes sounds. Your question translates to a series of sounds for him, and those sounds become the signal to go to you and pay attention; if he does, he will get to interact with you plus receive treats and praise.

THE BASIC COMMANDS

TEACHING SIT

Now that you have the dog's attention, attach his leash and hold it in your left hand and a

---

PRACTICE MAKES PERFECT!

- Have training lessons with your dog every day in several short segments—three to five times a day for a few minutes at a time is ideal.
- Do not have long practice sessions. The dog will become easily bored.
- Never practice when you are tired, ill, worried or in an otherwise negative mood. This will transmit to the dog and may have an adverse effect on his performance.

Think fun, short and above all *positive*! End each session on a high note, rather than a failed exercise, and make sure to give a lot of praise. Enjoy the training and help your dog enjoy it, too.

HONOR AND OBEY

Dogs are the most honorable animals in existence. They consider another species (humans) as their own. They interface with you. You are their leader. Puppies perceive children to be on their level; their actions around small children are different from their behavior around their adult masters.

food treat in your right. Place your food hand at the dog's nose and let him lick the treat but not take it from you. Say "Sit" and slowly raise your food hand from in front of the dog's nose up over his head so that he is looking at the ceiling. As he bends his head upward, he will have to bend his knees to maintain his balance. As he bends his

Housebreaking, teaching the rules and training the basic commands lay the foundations for your dog's daily routine and proper behavior.

knees, he will assume a sit position. At that point, release the food treat and praise lavishly with comments such as "Good dog! Good sit!," etc. Remember to always praise enthusiastically, because dogs relish verbal praise from their owners and feel so proud of themselves whenever they accomplish a behavior.

You will not use food forever in getting the dog to obey your commands. Food is only used to teach new behaviors, and once the dog knows what you want

Pekes require only light collars and leashes for training purposes.

HELPING PAWS
Your dog may not be the next Lassie, but every pet has the potential to do some tricks well. Identify his natural talents and hone them. Is your dog always happy and upbeat? Teach him to wag his tail or give you his paw on command. Real homebodies can be trained to do household chores, such as retrieving the morning paper.

when you give a specific command, you will wean him off the food treats but still maintain the verbal praise. After all, you will always have your voice with you, but there will be many times when you have no food rewards but expect the dog to obey.

TEACHING DOWN
Teaching the down exercise is easy when you understand how the dog perceives the down position, and it is very difficult when you do not. Dogs perceive the down position as a submissive one; therefore, teaching the down exercise using a forceful method can sometimes make the dog develop such a fear of the down that he either runs away when you say "Down" or he attempts to snap at the person who tries to force him down.

Have the dog sit close alongside your left leg, facing in the same direction as you are. Hold

Your Pekingese is a naturally beautiful dog. Your training ensures that his dignified behavior will befit his regal looks.

DOUBLE JEOPARDY

A dog in jeopardy never lies down. He stays alert on his feet because instinct tells him that he may have to run away or fight for his survival. Therefore, if a dog feels threatened or anxious, he will not lie down. Consequently, it is important to keep the dog calm and relaxed as he learns the down exercise.

spinal cord. Do not push down on the dog's shoulders; simply rest your left hand there so you can guide the dog to lie down close to your left leg rather than to swing away from your side when he drops.

Now place the food hand at the dog's nose, say "Down" very softly (almost a whisper) and slowly lower the food hand to the dog's front feet. When the food hand reaches the floor, begin moving it forward along the floor in front of the dog. Keep talking softly to the dog, saying things like, "Do you want this treat? You can do this, good dog." Your reassuring tone of voice will help calm the dog as he tries to follow the food hand in order to get the treat.

When the dog's elbows touch the floor, release the food and praise softly. Try to get the dog to maintain that down position for several seconds before you let him sit up again. The goal here is to get the dog to settle down and not feel threatened in the down position.

TEACHING STAY

It is easy to teach the dog to stay in either a sit or a down position. Again, we use food and praise during the teaching process as we help the dog to understand exactly what it is that we are expecting him to do.

To teach the sit/stay, start

the leash in your left hand and a food treat in your right. Now place your left hand lightly on the top of the dog's shoulders where they meet above the

Maltese

The Maltese, which originated on the Mediterranean island of Malta more than 28 centuries ago, has a gorgeous white silky coat that requires daily brushing and frequent bathing. Revered by the ancient Greeks, images of the breed appear on Greek ceramic art as early as the fifth century. Sweet, affectionate, and very playful, the Maltese bonds to one person and barks when anyone comes to the door.

Manchester Terrier (Toy)

This is the toy version of the Standard Manchester Terrier. Originally known in England as the Black-and-Tan Terrier, the breed has a warm and loyal personality and gets along well with other dogs.

Miniature Pinscher

Although they look like miniaturized Doberman Pinschers, the "Min Pin" is actually centuries older than the larger working dog. Despite their size—no taller than 12½ inches—these dogs are fearless and alert, making them ideal watchdogs.

Papillon

The name comes from the French word for *butterfly* because the breed's ears resemble butterfly wings. Ears may be either erect or drooping. The drop-eared variety is called a Phalene. Originally known as the Dwarf Spaniel, the Papillon appears in the paintings of many of the old masters, including Rubens, Velasquez, and Watteau. They were also favorites of ladies of the French court, such as Marie Antoinette and Madame de Pompadour. Despite their dainty appearance, Papillons are remarkably sturdy and excel in sports, such as obedience and agility.

Pekingese

Originally treasured by the ancient emperors of China, Pekingese were known as Lion Dogs, because of their leonine appearance, or Sun Dogs, because of their golden red coats. Another sobriquet was the "Sleeve Dog," because the tiniest specimens could be carried in the long sleeves of imperial household members. This breed has a long, elegant coat that requires a lot of brushing. Dignified and often aloof with strangers, Pekingese are very loyal to family members and bark when they sense danger.

Pomeranian

A small dog of the spitz family whose appearance hints at being descended from the sled dogs of Iceland and Lapland, the breed is outgoing and curious. Like their larger cousins, Pomeranians have fur to guard against the elements, consisting of a dense undercoat and a harsh-textured outer coat. Although most often seen in red or orange coats, they come in all colors, from white to dark brindle. Dog-loving Queen Victoria prized these canine companions. Her favorite, a Pomeranian named Turi, was at her side when she died.

Poodle (toy)

The national dog of France originated as a water retriever. The standard, miniature, and toy varieties are one breed, judged by the same breed standard. Poodles are highly intelligent, love to show off, and tend to bond to one person. While standard Poodles were famed as water retrievers, the smaller ones were useful in other jobs, such as circus performing and truffle-hunting. But like all Poodles, the toys are water dogs at heart, and most are enthusiastic swimmers. The word Poodle is said to have been derived from the German *pudel,* which means "to splash in water."

Pug

The largest of the toys, the Pug comes in two basic color varieties: all black or all fawn. The breed standard has a motto—*multum in parvo*—"a lot in a little." The elite in China and Europe favored the breed. In 1572, the Pug became the official dog of Holland's House of Orange, after one saved the life of William, Prince of Orange. Legend has it that another famous Pug, the pet of Napoleon's Josephine, bit the general on his wedding night.

with the dog sitting on your left side as before and hold the leash in your left hand. Have a food treat in your right hand and place your food hand at the dog's nose. Say "Stay" and step out on your right foot to stand directly in front of the dog, toe to toe, as he licks and nibbles the treat. Be sure to keep his head facing upward to maintain the sit position. Count to five and then swing around to stand next to the dog again with him on your left. As soon as you get back to the original position, release the food and praise lavishly.

To teach the down/stay, do the down as previously described. As soon as the dog lies down, say "Stay" and step out on your right foot just as you did in the sit/stay. Count to five and then return to stand beside the dog with him on your left side. Release the treat and praise as always.

Within a week or ten days, you can begin to add a bit of distance between you and your dog when you leave him. When you do, use your left hand open with the palm facing the dog as a stay signal, much the same as the hand signal a police officer uses to stop traffic at an intersection. Hold the food treat in your right hand as before, but this time the food is not touching the dog's nose. He will

watch the food hand and quickly learn that he is going to get that treat as soon as you return to his side.

When you can stand 1 yard away from your dog for 30 seconds, you can then begin building time and distance in both stays. Eventually, the dog can be expected to remain in the stay position for prolonged periods of time until you return to him or call him to you. Always praise lavishly when he stays.

FETCH!

Play fetching games with your puppy in an enclosed area where he can retrieve his toy and bring it back to you. Always use a toy or object designated just for this purpose. Never use a shoe, sock or other item he may later confuse with those in your closet or underneath your chair.

KEEP SMILING

Never train your dog, puppy or adult, when you are angry or in a sour mood. Dogs are very sensitive to human feelings, especially anger, and if your dog senses that you are angry or upset, he will connect your anger with his training and learn to resent or fear his training sessions.

TEACHING COME

If you make teaching "come" a fun experience, you should never have a student that does not love the game or that fails to come when called. The secret, it seems, is never to teach the word "come."

At times when an owner most wants his dog to come when called, the owner is likely upset or anxious and he allows these feelings to come through in the tone of his voice when he calls his dog. Hearing that desperation in his owner's voice, the dog fears the results of going to him and therefore either disobeys outright or runs in the opposite direction. The secret, therefore, is to teach the dog a game and, when you want him to come to you, simply play the game. It is practically a no-fail solution!

To begin, have several members of your family take a few food treats and each go into a different room in the house.

'What is this thing?' Before starting to teach any command, the pup must be accustomed to his leash.

Take turns calling the dog, and each person should celebrate the dog's finding him with a treat and lots of happy praise. When a person calls the dog, he is actually inviting the dog to find him and get a treat as a reward for "winning."

A few turns of the "Where are you?" game and the dog will understand that everyone is playing the game and that each person has a big celebration awaiting his success at locating him or her. Once he learns to love the game, simply calling out "Where are you?" will bring him running from wherever he is when he hears that all-important question.

The come command is recognized as one of the most important things to teach a dog, but there are trainers who work with thousands of dogs and never teach the actual word "come." Yet these dogs will race to respond to a person who uses the dog's name followed by "Where are you?" For example, a woman has a 12-year-old companion dog who went blind, but who never fails to locate her owner when asked, "Where are you?"

Children particularly love to play this game with their dogs. Children can hide in smaller places like a shower stall or bathtub, behind a bed or under a table. The dog needs to work a little bit harder to find these hiding places, but when he does he loves to celebrate with a treat and a tussle with a favorite youngster.

"COME" . . . BACK

Never call your dog to come to you for a correction or scold him when he reaches you. That is the quickest way to turn a come command into "Go away fast!" Dogs think only in the present tense, and your dog will connect the scolding with coming to you, not with the misbehavior of a few moments earlier.

TEACHING HEEL

Heeling means that the dog walks beside the owner without pulling. It takes time and patience on the owner's part to succeed at teaching the dog that he (the owner) will not proceed unless the dog is walking calmly beside him. Pulling out ahead on the leash is definitely not acceptable.

Begin with holding the leash in your left hand as the dog sits beside your left leg. Move the loop end of the leash to your right hand but keep your left

Your dog should snap to attention whenever he hears his name and "Where are you?"

close to you and take three steps. Stop and have the dog sit next to you in what we now call the heel position. Praise verbally, but do not touch the dog. Hesitate a moment and begin again with "Heel," taking three steps and stopping, at which point the dog is told to sit again.

Your goal here is to have the dog walk those three steps without pulling on the leash. When he will walk calmly beside you for three steps without pulling, increase the number of steps you take to five. When he will walk politely beside you while you take five steps, you can increase the length of your walk to ten steps. Keep increasing the length of your stroll until the dog will walk quietly beside you without pulling as long as you want him to heel. When you stop heeling, indicate to the dog that the exercise is over by verbally praising as you pet him and say, "OK, good dog." The "OK" is used as a release word, meaning that the exercise is finished and the dog is free to relax.

If you are dealing with a dog who insists on pulling you around, simply "put on your brakes" and stand your ground until the dog realizes that the two of you are not going anywhere until he is beside you and moving at your pace, not his. It may take some time just

TUG OF WALK?

If you begin teaching the heel by taking long walks and letting the dog pull you along, he misinterprets this action as an acceptable form of taking a walk. When you pull back on the leash to counteract his pulling, he reads that tug as a signal to pull even harder!

hand short on the leash so that it keeps the dog in close next to you.

Say "Heel" and step forward on your left foot. Keep the dog

standing there to convince the dog that you are the leader and you will be the one to decide on the direction and speed of your travel.

Each time the dog looks up at you or slows down to give a slack leash between the two of you, quietly praise him and say, "Good heel. Good dog." Eventually, the dog will begin to respond and within a few days he will be walking politely beside you without pulling on the leash. At first, the training sessions should be kept short and very positive; soon the dog will be able to walk nicely with you for increasingly longer distances. Remember also to give the dog free time and the opportunity to run and play when you have finished heel practice.

WEANING OFF FOOD IN TRAINING

Food is used in training new behaviors. Once the dog understands what behavior goes with a specific command, it is time to start weaning him off the food treats. At first, give a treat after each exercise. Then, start to give a treat only after every other exercise. Vary the times when you offer a food reward and the times when you only offer praise so that the dog will never know when he is going to receive both food and praise and when he is going to receive only praise.

THE STUDENT'S STRESS TEST

During training sessions, you must be able to recognize signs of stress in your dog such as:

- tucking his tail between his legs
- lowering his head
- shivering or trembling
- standing completely still or running away
- panting and/or salivating
- avoiding eye contact
- flattening his ears back
- urinating submissively
- rolling over and lifting a leg
- grinning or baring teeth
- aggression when restrained

If your four-legged student displays these signs, he may just be nervous or intimidated. The training session may have been too lengthy, with not enough praise and affirmation. Stop for the day and try again tomorrow.

This is called a variable-ratio reward system and it proves successful because there is always the chance that the owner will produce a treat, so the dog never stops trying for that reward. No matter what, *always* give verbal praise.

OBEDIENCE CLASSES

It is a good idea to enroll in an obedience class if one is available in your area. If yours is a show dog, classes to prepare for the show ring would be more appropriate. Many areas have dog clubs that offer basic obedience training as well as prepara-

In advanced obedience exercises, the dog must respond to hand signals given by his owner.

SAFETY FIRST
While it may seem that the most important things to your dog are eating, sleeping and chewing the upholstery on your furniture, his first concern is actually safety. The domesticated dogs we keep as companions have the same pack instinct as their ancestors who ran free thousands of years ago. Because of this pack instinct, your dog wants to know that he and his pack are not in danger of being harmed, and that his pack has a strong, capable leader. You must establish yourself as the leader early on in your relationship. That way your dog will trust that you will take care of him and the pack, and he will accept your commands without question.

tory classes for obedience competition. There are also local dog trainers who offer similar classes.

At obedience trials, dogs can earn titles at various levels of competition. The beginning levels of competition include basic behaviors such as sit, down, heel, etc. The more advanced levels of competition include jumping, retrieving, scent discrimination and signal work. The advanced levels require a dog and owner to put a lot of time and effort into their training and the titles that can be earned at these levels of competition are very prestigious.

OTHER ACTIVITIES FOR LIFE

Whether a dog is trained in a class or with his owner at home, there are many activities that can bring fun and rewards to both owner and dog once they have mastered basic control.

Teaching the dog to help out around the home or in the yard provides great satisfaction to both dog and owner. In addition, the dog's help makes life a little easier for his owner and raises his stature as a valued companion to his family. It helps to give the dog a purpose by occupying his mind and providing an outlet for his energy.

If you are interested in participating in organized competition with your Pekingese, there are activities other than obedience in which you and your dog can become involved. Agility is a popular sport where dogs run through an obstacle course that includes various jumps, tunnels and other exercises to test the dog's speed and coordination. Small breeds can participate just as larger dogs can, as the obstacles are reduced in size to be proportionate to the smaller breeds' size. The owners run through the course beside their dogs to give commands and to guide them through the course. Although competitive, the focus is on fun—it's fun to do, fun to watch and great exercise.

HOW TO WEAN THE "TREAT HOG"

If you have trained your dog by rewarding him with a treat each time he performs a command, he may soon decide that without the treat, he won't sit, stay or come. The best way to fix this problem is to start asking your dog to do certain commands twice before being rewarded. Slowly increase the number of commands given and then vary the number: three sits and a treat one day, five sits for a biscuit the next day, etc. Your dog will soon realize that there is no set number of sits before he gets his reward and he'll likely do it the first time you ask in the hope of being rewarded sooner rather than later.

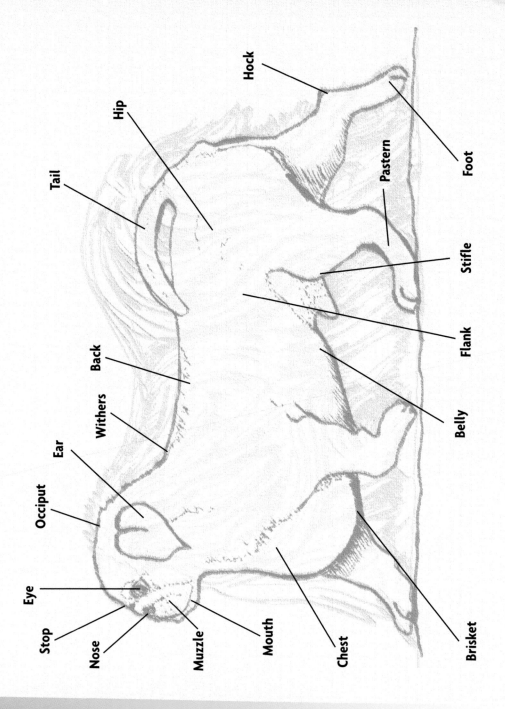

Physical Structure of the Pekingese

PEKINGESE

Dogs suffer from many of the same physical illnesses as people. They might even share many of the same psychological problems. Since people usually know more about human diseases than canine maladies, many of the terms used in this chapter will be familiar but not necessarily those used by veterinarians. We will use the term *x-ray*, instead of the more acceptable term *radiograph*. We will also use the familiar term *symptoms* even though dogs don't have symptoms, which are verbal descriptions of the patient's feelings; instead, dogs have *clinical signs*. Since dogs can't speak, we have to look for clinical signs...but we still use the term *symptoms* in this book.

As a general rule, medicine is practiced. That term is not arbitrary. Medicine is a constantly changing art as we learn more and more about genetics, electronic aids (like CAT scans and MRIs) and daily laboratory advances. There are many dog maladies, like hip dysplasia, that are not universally treated in the same manner. For example, some veterinarians opt for surgery more often than others do.

SELECTING A QUALIFIED VET

Your selection of a veterinarian should be based not only upon his personality and skills but also upon his convenience to your home. You want a vet who is close because you might have emergencies or need to make multiple visits for treatments. You want a vet who has services that you might require such as grooming facilities, boarding and tattooing, and, most importantly, a good reputation for ability and responsiveness.

There is nothing more frustrating than having to wait to get a response from your veterinarian.

All vets are licensed and should be capable of dealing with

Before you buy a dog, meet and interview the vets in your area. Take everything into consideration; discuss background, specialties, fees, emergency policies, etc.

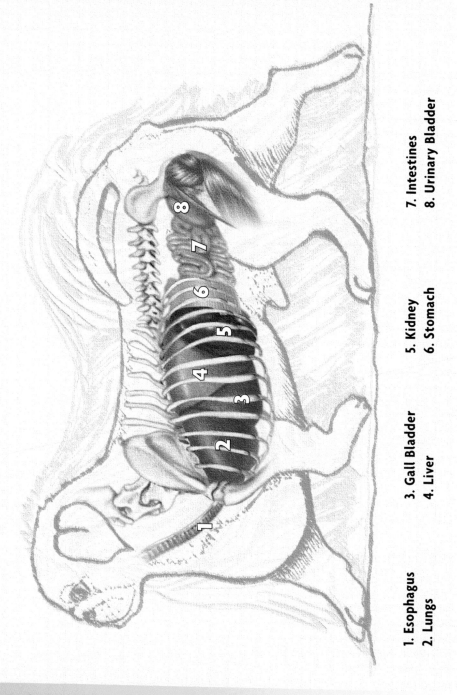

1. Esophagus
2. Lungs

3. Gall Bladder
4. Liver

5. Kidney
6. Stomach

7. Intestines
8. Urinary Bladder

Internal Organs of the Pekingese

routine medical issues such as injuries, infections and promotion of health (for example, by vaccination). Most vets do routine surgery such as neutering, stitching up wounds and docking tails for those breeds in which such is required for show purposes. If the problem affecting your Peke is more serious, your vet will refer your pet to a specialist who concentrates in the relevant field (such as veterinary dermatology, ophthalmology, oncolgy, etc.).

When the problem affecting your dog is serious, it is not unusual or impudent to get another medical opinion, although it is courteous to advise the vets concerned about this. You might also want to compare costs among several veterinarians. Sophisticated health care and veterinary services can be very costly. Don't be bashful about discussing these costs with your vet. If there is more than one treatment option, cost may be a factor in deciding which route to take. Veterinary insurance is becoming more common; investigate the types of policies available to pet owners.

Breakdown of Veterinary Income by Category

2%	Dentistry
4%	Radiology
12%	Surgery
15%	Vaccinations
19%	Laboratory
23%	Examinations
25%	Medicines

A typical vet's income, categorized according to services performed. This survey dealt with small-animal (pets) practices.

PREVENTATIVE MEDICINE

It is much easier, less costly and more effective to practice preventative medicine than to fight bouts of illness and disease. Properly bred puppies come from parents that were selected based upon their genetic-disease profiles. Their mother should have been vaccinated, free of all internal and external parasites and properly nourished. For these reasons, a visit to the vet who cared for the dam is recommended. The dam can pass on disease resistance to her puppies, which can last for eight to ten weeks. She can also pass on parasites and many infections. That's why it's helpful to know as much as possible about her health.

NEUTERING/SPAYING

Male dogs are castrated. The operation removes both testicles and requires that the dog be anesthetized. Recovery takes about one week. Females are spayed; in this operation, the uterus (womb) and both of the ovaries are removed. This is major surgery, also carried out under general anesthesia, and it usually takes a bitch two weeks to recover.

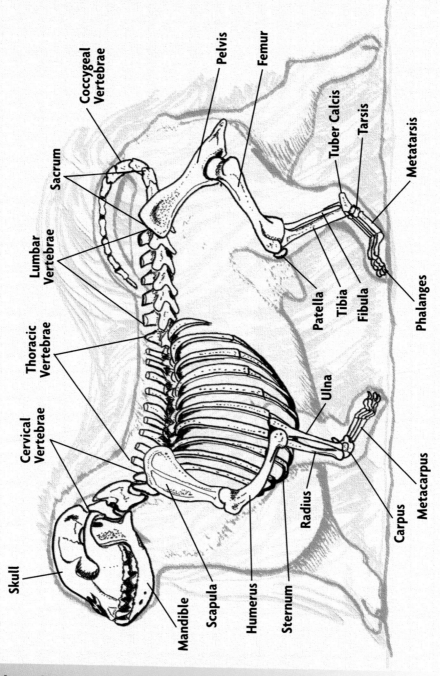

Coccygeal Vertebrae

Pelvis

Femur

Tuber Calcis

Tarsis

Metatarsis

Sacrum

Lumbar Vertebrae

Patella

Tibia

Fibula

Phalanges

Thoracic Vertebrae

Ulna

Cervical Vertebrae

Radius

Carpus

Metacarpus

Skull

Mandible

Scapula

Humerus

Sternum

Skeletal Structure of the Pekingese

MORE THAN VACCINES

Vaccinations help prevent your new puppy from contracting diseases, but they do not cure them. Proper nutrition as well as parasite control keep your dog healthy and less susceptible to many dangerous diseases. Remember that your dog depends on you to ensure his well-being.

WEANING TO FIVE MONTHS OLD

Puppies should be weaned by the time they are about two months old. A puppy that remains for at least eight weeks with his mother and littermates usually adapts better to other dogs and people later in his life.

Sometimes new owners have their puppy examined by a vet immediately, which is a good idea unless the pup is overtired by a long journey home from the breeder's. In this case, an appointment should be made for the next day or two.

The puppy will have his teeth examined and have his skeletal conformation and general health checked prior to certification by the vet. Puppies in certain breeds have problems with their kneecaps, cataracts and other eye problems, heart murmurs and undescended testicles. Your vet might also have training in temperament evaluation and can advise you about your youngster's personality. At the first visit, the vet will set up a schedule for your pup's vaccinations.

VACCINATION SCHEDULING

Most vaccinations are given by injection and should only be done by a vet. Both he and you should keep a record of the date of the injection, the identification of the vaccine and the amount given. Some vets give a first vaccination around six weeks, but most dog breeders prefer the course not to commence until about eight weeks because of the risk of negating antibodies passed on by the dam. The scheduling is usually based on a two- to four-week cycle. You must take your vet's advice as to when to vaccinate as this may differ according to the vaccine used.

Most vaccinations immunize your puppy against viruses. The usual vaccines contain immunizing doses of several different viruses such as distemper, parvovirus, parainfluenza and hepatitis. There are other vaccines available when the puppy is at risk. You should always rely upon professional advice. This is especially true for the booster-shot program. Most vaccination programs require a booster when the puppy is a year old and once a year thereafter. In some cases, circumstances may require more or less frequent immunizations.

Canine cough, more formally known as tracheobronchitis, is treated with a vaccine that is sprayed into the dog's nostrils. Canine cough is usually included in routine vaccination, but this is often not so effective as for other major diseases.

HEALTH AND VACCINATION SCHEDULE

Age in Weeks:	6th	8th	10th	12th	14th	16th	20-24th	52nd
Worm Control	✔	✔	✔	✔	✔	✔	✔	
Neutering							✔	
Heartworm		✔		✔		✔	✔	
Parvovirus	✔		✔		✔		✔	✔
Distemper		✔		✔		✔		✔
Hepatitis		✔		✔		✔		✔
Leptospirosis								✔
Parainfluenza	✔		✔		✔			✔
Dental Examination		✔					✔	✔
Complete Physical		✔					✔	✔
Coronavirus				✔			✔	✔
Canine Cough	✔							
Hip Dysplasia								✔
Rabies							✔	

Vaccinations are not instantly effective. It takes about two weeks for the dog's immune system to develop antibodies. Most vaccinations require annual booster shots. Your vet should guide you in this regard.

FIVE TO TWELVE MONTHS OF AGE

Unless you intend to breed or show your dog, neutering the puppy by six months of age is recommended. Discuss this with your vet; most professionals advise neutering the puppy. Neutering/spaying has proven to be extremely beneficial to male and female puppies, respectively. Besides eliminating the possibility of pregnancy, it greatly decreases the risk of breast cancer in bitches and prostate cancer in male dogs, and eliminates the risk of testicular cancer in males and pyometra in females. It is very rare to diagnose breast cancer in a bitch who was spayed at or before her first heat.

Your vet should provide your puppy with a thorough dental evaluation at six months of age, ascertaining whether all of the permanent teeth have erupted properly. A home dental-care regimen should be initiated at six months, including brushing weekly and providing good dental devices (such as nylon bones). Regular dental care promotes healthy teeth, fresh breath and a longer life.

DOGS OLDER THAN ONE YEAR

Once a year, your grown dog should visit the vet for an examination and vaccination boosters. Some vets recommend blood tests, thyroid level check and

VACCINE ALLERGIES

Vaccines do not work all the time. Sometimes dogs are allergic to them and many times the antibodies, which are supposed to be stimulated by the vaccine, just are not produced. You should keep your dog in the veterinary clinic for an hour after it is vaccinated to be sure there are no allergic reactions.

dental evaluation to accompany these annual visits. A thorough clinical evaluation by the vet can provide critical background information for your dog. Blood tests are often performed at one year of age, and dental examinations around the third or fourth birthday. In the long run, quality preventive care for your pet can save money, teeth and lives.

SKIN PROBLEMS IN PEKINGESE

Veterinarians are consulted by dog owners for skin problems more than any for other group of diseases or maladies. Dogs' skin is almost as sensitive as humans' skin and both can suffer from almost the same ailments, though the occurrence of acne in most

DISEASE REFERENCE CHART

	What is it?	What causes it?	Symptoms
Leptospirosis	Severe disease that affects the internal organs; can be spread to people.	A bacterium, which is often carried by rodents, that enters through mucous membranes and spreads quickly throughout the body.	Range from fever, vomiting and loss of appetite in less severe cases to shock, irreversible kidney damage and possibly death in most severe cases.
Rabies	Potentially deadly virus that infects warm-blooded mammals.	Bite from a carrier of the virus, mainly wild animals.	1st stage: dog exhibits change in behavior, fear. 2nd stage: dog's behavior becomes more aggressive. 3rd stage: loss of coordination, trouble with bodily functions.
Parvovirus	Highly contagious virus, potentially deadly.	Ingestion of the virus, which is usually spread through the feces of infected dogs.	Most common: severe diarrhea. Also vomiting, fatigue, lack of appetite.
Canine cough	Contagious respiratory infection.	Combination of types of bacteria and virus. Most common: *Bordetella bronchiseptica* bacteria and parainfluenza virus.	Chronic cough.
Distemper	Disease primarily affecting respiratory and nervous system.	Virus that is related to the human measles virus.	Mild symptoms such as fever, lack of appetite and mucus secretion progress to evidence of brain damage, "hard pad."
Hepatitis	Virus primarily affecting the liver.	Canine adenovirus type I (CAV-1). Enters system when dog breathes in particles.	Lesser symptoms include listlessness, diarrhea, vomiting. More severe symptoms include "blue-eye" (clumps of virus in eye).
Coronavirus	Virus resulting in digestive problems.	Virus is spread through infected dog's feces.	Stomach upset evidenced by lack of appetite, vomiting, diarrhea.

KNOW WHEN TO POSTPONE A VACCINATION

While the visit to the vet is costly, it is never advisable to update a vaccination when visiting with a sick or pregnant dog. Vaccinations also should be avoided for all elderly dogs. If your dog is showing the signs of any illness or any medical condition, no matter how serious or mild, including skin irritations, do not vaccinate. Likewise, a lame dog should never be vaccinated, and any dog undergoing surgery or on any immuno-suppressant drugs should not be vaccinated until fully recovered.

dogs is rare. For this reason, veterinary dermatology has developed into a specialty practiced by many vets.

Since many skin problems have visual symptoms that are almost identical, it requires the skill of an experienced veterinary dermatologist to identify and cure many of the more severe skin disorders. Pet shops sell many treatments for skin problems, but most of the treatments are directed at symptoms and not the underlying problem(s). If your dog is suffering from a skin disorder, you should seek professional assistance as quickly as possible. As with all diseases, the earlier a problem is identified and treated, the more likely it is that the cure will be successful.

HEREDITARY SKIN DISORDERS

Veterinary dermatologists are currently researching a number of skin disorders that are believed to have hereditary bases. These inherited diseases are transmitted by both parents, who appear (phenotypically) normal but have a recessive gene for the disease, meaning that they carry, but are not affected by, the disease. These disease pose serious problems to breeders because in some instances there are no methods of identifying carriers. Often the secondary diseases associated with these skin conditions are even more debilitating than the skin disorder, including cancers and respiratory problems.

Among the known hereditary skin disorders, for which the mode of inheritance is known, are acrodermatitis, cutaneous asthenia (Ehlers-Danlos syndrome), sebaceous adenitis, cyclic hematopoiesis, dermatomyositis, IgA deficiency, color dilution alopecia and nodular dermatofibrosis. Some of these disorders are limited to one or two breeds and others affect a large number of breeds. All inherited diseases must be diagnosed and treated by a veterinary specialist.

PARASITE BITES

Many of us are allergic to insect bites. The bites itch, erupt and may even become infected. Dogs have the same reaction to fleas, ticks and/or mites. When an insect lands on you, you have the chance to whisk it away with your hand. Unfortunately, when your dog is bitten by a flea, tick or mite, he can only scratch it away or bite it. By the time the dog has been bitten, the parasite has done some of its damage. It may also have laid eggs, which will cause further problems in the near future. The itching from parasite bites is probably due to the saliva injected into the site when the parasite sucks the dog's blood.

AIRBORNE ALLERGIES

Just as humans have hay fever, rose fever and other fevers with which they suffer during the pollinating season, many dogs suffer from the same allergies. When the pollen count is high, your dog might suffer, but don't expect him to sneeze and have a runny nose like a human would. Dogs react to pollen allergies the same way they react to fleas—they scratch and bite themselves.

Dogs, like humans, can be tested for allergens. Discuss the testing with your veterinary dermatologist.

SKIN ALLERGIES

Like many other breeds, some Pekingese are prone to allergies, but these can often be kept under control with a carefully considered diet. The allergy might be noticed as "hot spots" on the skin,

despite there being no sign of external parasites. A low-protein diet often seems to alleviate skin troubles, and ideally one should try to identify and eliminate any foods that are causing or exacerbating the problem.

Indeed, it is often extremely difficult to ascertain the cause of the allergy. There are many possibilities, ranging from the living room carpet to the shampoo used when bathing to, quite frequently, certain grasses and molds. In cases of skin allergy, it is a good

CARETAKER OF TEETH

You are your dog's caretaker and his dentist. Vets warn that plaque and tartar buildup on the teeth will damage the gums and allow bacteria to enter the dog's bloodstream, causing serious damage to the animal's vital organs. Studies show that over 50 percent of dogs have some form of gum disease before age three. Daily or weekly tooth cleaning (with a brush or soft gauze pad wipes) can add to your dog's life.

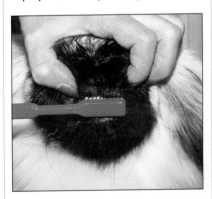

Don't Eat the Daisies!

Many plants and flowers are beautiful to look at, but can be highly toxic if ingested by your dog. Reactions range from abdominal pain and vomiting to convulsions and death. If the following plants are in your home, remove them. If they are outside your house or in your garden, avoid accidents by removing them or making sure your dog is never left unsupervised in those locations.

Azalea	Dumb cane	Mescal bean
Belladonna	Dutchman's breeches	Mushrooms
Bird of paradise	Elephant's ear	Nightshade
Bulbs	Hydrangea	Philodendron
Calla lily	Jack-in-the-pulpit	Poinsettia
Cardinal flower	Jasmine	*Prunus* species
Castor bean	Jimsonweed	Tobacco
Chinaberry tree	Larkspur	Yellow jasmine
Daphne	Laurel	Yews, *Taxus* species
	Lily of the valley	

idea to change shampoo, conditioning rinse and any other coat sprays used, for these are perhaps the easiest items to eliminate before looking further if necessary. It goes without saying that your Pekingese must be kept free of external parasites such as fleas.

AUTO-IMMUNE ILLNESSES

An auto-immune illness is one in which the immune system overacts and does not recognize parts of the affected person or dog; rather, the immune system starts to react as if these parts were foreign and need to be destroyed. An example is rheumatoid arthritis, which occurs when the body does not recognize the joints, thus leading to a very painful and damaging reaction in the joints. This has nothing to do with age, so can occur in children and young dogs. The wear-and-tear arthritis of the older person or dog is osteoarthritis.

Lupus is an auto-immune disease that affects dogs as well as people. It can take variable forms, affecting the kidneys, bones and the skin. It can be fatal, so is treated with steroids, which can themselves have very significant side effects. The steroids calm down the allergic reaction to the body's tissues, which helps the lupus, but the steroids also calm down the body's reaction to real foreign substances such as bacteria, and also thin the skin and bones.

FOOD PROBLEMS

FOOD ALLERGIES
Some dogs can be allergic to many foods that
may be best-sellers and highly recommended by breeders and vets. Changing the brand of food that you buy may not eliminate the problem if the element to which the dog is allergic is contained in the new brand.

Recognizing a food allergy in a dog can be difficult. Humans often have rashes when they eat foods to which they are allergic, or have swelling of the lips or eyes. Dogs do not usually develop rashes, but react in the same way as they do to an airborne or bite allergy—-they itch, scratch and bite. While pollen allergies are usually seasonal, food allergies are year-round problems.

TREATING FOOD ALLERGY
Diagnosis of food allergy is based on a two- to four-week dietary trial with a home-cooked diet fed to the exclusion of all other foods. The diet should consist of boiled rice or potato with a source of protein that the dog has never eaten before, such as fresh or frozen fish, lamb or even something as exotic as pheasant or ostrich (if this is not too expensive in your part of the country). Water has to be the only drink, and it is really important that no other foods are fed during this trial. If the dog's condition improves, you will need to try the original diet once again to see if the itching resumes. If it does, then this confirms the diagnosis that the dog is allergic to his original diet. The treatment is long-term feeding of something that does not distress the dog's skin, which may be in the form of one of the commercially available hypoallergenic diets or the home-made diet that you created for the allergy trial.

FOOD INTOLERANCE
Food intolerance is the inability of the dog to completely digest certain foods. This occurs because the dog does not have the chemicals necessary to digest some foodstuffs. These chemicals are called enzymes. All puppies have the enzymes necessary to digest canine milk, but some dogs do not have the enzymes to digest a very different form of milk—milk from cows. In such dogs, drinking cows' milk results in loose bowels, stomach pains and the passage of gas.

Dogs often do not have the enzymes to digest soy or other beans. The treatment is to exclude the foodstuffs that upset your Peke's digestion.

A male dog flea,
Ctenocephalides
canis.

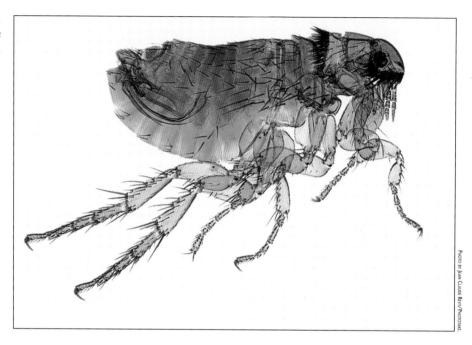

PHOTO BY JEAN CLAUDE REVY/PHOTOTAKE.

EXTERNAL PARASITES

FLEAS

Of all the problems to which dogs are prone, none is more well known and frustrating than fleas. Flea infestation is relatively simple to cure but difficult to prevent. Parasites that are harbored inside the body are a bit more difficult to eradicate but they are easier to control.

To control flea infestation, you have to understand the flea's life cycle. Fleas are often thought of as a summertime problem, but centrally heated homes have changed the patterns and fleas can be found at any time of the year. The most effective method of flea control is a two-stage approach: one stage to kill the adult fleas, and the other to control the development of pre-adult fleas. Unfortunately, no single active ingredient is effective against all stages of the life cycle.

FLEA KILLER CAUTION—"POISON"

Flea-killers are poisonous. You should not spray these toxic chemicals on areas of a dog's body that he licks, including his genitals and his face. Flea killers taken internally are a better answer, but check with your vet in case internal therapy is not advised for your dog.

LIFE CYCLE STAGES

During its life, a flea will pass through four life stages: egg, larva, pupa or nymph and adult. The adult stage is the most visible and irritating stage of the flea life cycle, and this is why the majority of flea-control products concentrate on this stage. The fact is that adult fleas account for only 1% of the total flea population, and the other 99% exist in pre-adult stages, i.e., eggs, larvae and nymphs. The pre-adult stages are barely visible to the naked eye.

THE LIFE CYCLE OF THE FLEA

Eggs are laid on the dog, usually in quantities of about 20 or 30, several times a day. The adult female flea must have a blood meal before each egg-laying session. When first laid, the eggs will cling to the dog's hair, as the eggs are still moist. However, they will quickly dry out and fall from the dog, especially if the dog moves around or scratches. Many eggs will fall off in the dog's favorite area or an area in which he spends a lot of time, such as his bed.

Once the eggs fall from the dog onto the carpet or furniture, they will hatch into larvae. This takes from one to ten days. Larvae are not particularly mobile and will usually travel only a few inches from where they hatch. However, they do have a tendency to move away from bright light and heavy

EN GARDE:
CATCHING FLEAS OFF GUARD!
Consider the following ways to arm yourself against fleas:
- Add a small amount of pennyroyal or eucalyptus oil to your dog's bath. These natural remedies repel fleas.
- Supplement your dog's food with fresh garlic (minced or grated) and a hearty amount of brewer's yeast, both of which ward off fleas.
- Use a flea comb on your dog daily. Submerge fleas in a cup of bleach to kill them quickly.
- Confine the dog to only a few rooms to limit the spread of fleas in the home.
- Vacuum daily...and get all of the crevices! Dispose of the bag every few days until the problem is under control.
- Wash your dog's bedding daily. Cover cushions where your dog sleeps with towels, and wash the towels often.

traffic—under furniture and behind doors are common places to find high quantities of flea larvae.

The flea larvae feed on dead organic matter, including adult flea feces, until they are ready to change into adult fleas. Fleas will usually remain as larvae for around seven days. After this period, the larvae will pupate into protective pupae. While inside the pupae, the larvae will undergo

Fleas have been measured as being able to jump 300,000 times and can jump over 150 times their length in any direction, including straight up.

metamorphosis and change into adult fleas. This can take as little time as a few days, but the adult fleas can remain inside the pupae waiting to hatch for up to two years. The pupae are signaled to hatch by certain stimuli, such as physical pressure—the pupae's being stepped on, heat from an animal's lying on the pupae or increased carbon-dioxide levels and vibrations—indicating that a suitable host is available.

Once hatched, the adult flea must feed within a few days. Once the adult flea finds a host, it will not leave voluntarily. It only becomes dislodged by grooming or the host animal's scratching.

The adult flea will remain on the host for the duration of its life unless forcibly removed.

TREATING THE ENVIRONMENT AND THE DOG

Treating fleas should be a two-pronged attack. First, the environment needs to be treated; this includes carpets and furniture, especially the dog's bedding and areas underneath furniture. The environment should be treated with a household spray containing an Insect Growth Regulator (IGR) and an insecticide to kill the adult fleas. Most IGRs are effective against eggs and larvae; they actually mimic the fleas' own hormones and stop the eggs and larvae from developing into adult fleas. There are currently no treatments available to attack the pupa stage of the life cycle, so the adult insecticide is used to kill the newly hatched adult fleas before they find a host. Most IGRs are active for many months, while

A scanning electron micrograph of a dog or cat flea, *Ctenocephalides*, magnified more than 100x. This image has been colorized for effect.

THE LIFE CYCLE OF THE FLEA

Adult

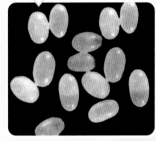

Egg

**Pupa
or
Nymph**

Larva

Fleas have been around for millions of years and have adapted to changing host animals. They are able to go through a complete life cycle in less than one month or they can extend their lives to almost two years by remaining as pupae or cocoons. They do not need blood or any other food for up to 20 months.

INSECT GROWTH REGULATOR (IGR)

Two types of products should be used when treating fleas—a product to treat the pet and a product to treat the home. Adult fleas represent less than 1% of the flea population. The pre-adult fleas (eggs, larvae and pupae) represent more than 99% of the flea population and are found in the environment; it is in the case of pre-adult fleas that products containing an Insect Growth Regulator (IGR) should be used in the home.

IGRs are a new class of compounds used to prevent the development of insects. They do not kill the insect outright, but instead use the insect's biology against it to stop it from completing its growth. Products that contain methoprene are the world's first and leading IGRs. Used to control fleas and other insects, this type of IGR will stop flea larvae from developing and protect the house for up to seven months.

The American dog tick, *Dermacentor variabilis*, is probably the most common tick found on dogs. Look at the strength in its eight legs! No wonder it's hard to detach them.

adult insecticides are only active for a few days.

When treating with a household spray, it is a good idea to vacuum before applying the product. This stimulates as many pupae as possible to hatch into adult fleas. The vacuum cleaner should also be treated with an insecticide to prevent the eggs and larvae that have been collected in the vacuum bag from hatching.

The second stage of treatment is to apply an adult insecticide to the dog. Traditionally, this would be in the form of a collar or a spray, but more recent innovations include digestible insecticides that poison the fleas when they ingest the dog's blood. Alternatively, there are drops that, when placed on the back of the dog's neck, spread throughout the hair and skin to kill adult fleas.

TICKS

Though not as common as fleas, ticks are found all over the tropical and temperate world. They don't bite, like fleas; they harpoon. They dig their sharp proboscis (nose) into the dog's skin and drink the blood. Their

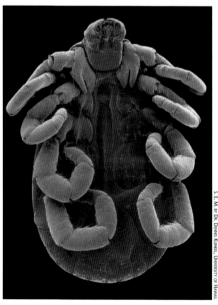

only food and drink is dog's blood. Dogs can get Lyme disease, Rocky Mountain spotted fever, tick bite paralysis and many other diseases from ticks. They may live where fleas are found and they like to hide in cracks or seams in walls. They are controlled the same way fleas are controlled.

The American dog tick, *Dermacentor variabilis*, may well be the most common dog tick in many geographical areas, especially those areas where the climate is hot and humid. Most dog ticks have life expectancies of a week to six months, depending upon climatic conditions. They can neither jump nor fly, but they can crawl slowly and can range up to 16 feet to reach a sleeping or unsuspecting dog.

MITES

Just as fleas and ticks can be problematic for your dog, mites can also lead to an itchy nuisance. Microscopic in size, mites are related to ticks and generally take up permanent residence on their host animal—in this case, your dog! The term *mange* refers to any infestation caused by one of the mighty mites, of which there are six varieties that concern dog owners.

Demodex mites cause a condition known as demodicosis

DEER-TICK CROSSING

The great outdoors may be fun for your dog, but it also is a home to dangerous ticks. Deer ticks carry a bacterium known as *Borrelia burgdorferi* and are most active in the autumn and spring. When infections are caught early, penicillin and tetracycline are effective antibiotics, but, if left untreated, the bacteria may cause neurological, kidney and cardiac problems as well as long-term trouble with walking and painful joints.

S. E. M. BY DR. ANDREW SPIELMAN/PHOTOTAKE.

PHOTO BY DR. DENNIS KUNKEL, UNIVERSITY OF HAWAII.

The head of an American dog tick, *Dermacentor variabilis*, enlarged and colorized for effect.

The mange mite, *Psoroptes bovis*, can infest cattle and other domestic animals.

PHOTO BY JAMES HAYDEN/YOAV/PHOTOTAKE.

Human lice look like dog lice; the two are closely related.

PHOTO BY DWIGHT R. KUHN.

(sometimes called red mange or follicular mange), in which the mites live in the dog's hair follicles and sebaceous glands in larger-than-normal numbers. This type of mange is commonly passed from the dam to her puppies and usually shows up on the puppies' muzzles, though demodicosis is not transferable from one normal dog to another. Most dogs recover from this type of mange without any treatment, though topical therapies are commonly prescribed by the vet.

The *Cheyletiellosis* mite is the hook-mouthed culprit associated with "walking dandruff," a condition that affects dogs as well as cats and rabbits. This mite lives on the surface of the animal's skin and is readily transferable through direct or indirect contact with an affected animal. The dandruff is present in the form of scaly skin, which may or may not be itchy. If not treated, this mange can affect a whole kennel of dogs and can be spread to humans as well.

The *Sarcoptes* mite causes intense itching on the dog in the form of a condition known as scabies or sarcoptic mange. The cycle of the *Sarcoptes* mite lasts about three weeks, and the mites live in the top layer of the dog's skin (epidermis), preferably in areas with little hair. Scabies is highly contagious and can be passed to humans. Sometimes an allergic reaction to the mite worsens the severe itching associated with sarcoptic mange.

Ear mites, *Otodectes cynotis,* lead to otodectic mange, which most commonly affects the outer ear canal of the dog, though other areas can be affected as well. Dogs with ear-mite infestation commonly scratch at their ears, causing further irritation, and shake their heads. Dark brown droppings in the outer ear confirm the diagnosis. Your vet can prescribe a treatment to flush out the ears and kill any eggs in the ears. A complete month of treatment is necessary to cure the mange.

Two other mites, less common in dogs, include *Dermanyssus gallinae* (the poultry or red mite) and *Eutrombicula alfreddugesi* (the North American mite associated with trombiculidiasis or chigger infestation). The poultry mite frequently lives on chickens, but can transfer to dogs who spend time near farm animals. Chigger infestation affects dogs in the

DO NOT MIX
Never mix parasite-control products without first consulting your vet. Some products can become toxic when combined with others and can cause fatal consequences.

NOT A DROP TO DRINK
Never allow your dog to swim in polluted water or public areas where water quality can be suspect. Even perfectly clear water can harbor parasites, many of which can cause serious to fatal illnesses in canines. Areas inhabited by waterfowl and other wildlife are especially dangerous.

Central US who have exposure to woodlands. The types of mange caused by both of these mites are treatable by vets.

INTERNAL PARASITES

Most animals—fishes, birds and mammals, including dogs and humans—have worms and other parasites that live inside their bodies. According to Dr. Herbert R. Axelrod, the fish pathologist, there are two kinds of parasites: dumb and smart. The smart parasites live in peaceful cooperation with their hosts (symbiosis), while the dumb parasites kill their hosts. Most worm infections are relatively easy to control. If they are not controlled, they weaken the host dog to the point that other medical problems occur, but they do not kill the host as dumb parasites would.

A brown dog tick, *Rhipicephalus sanguineus*, is an uncommon but annoying tick found on dogs.
PHOTO BY CAROLINA BIOLOGICAL SUPPLY/PHOTOTAKE.

The roundworm *Rhabditis* can infect both dogs and humans.

ROUNDWORMS

Average-size dogs can pass 1,360,000 roundworm eggs every day. For example, if there were only 1 million dogs in the world, the world would be saturated with thousands of tons of dog feces. These feces would contain around 15,000,000,000 roundworm eggs.

Up to 31% of home yards and children's sand boxes in the US contain roundworm eggs.

Flushing dog's feces down the toilet is not a safe practice because the usual sewage treatments do not destroy roundworm eggs.

Infected puppies start shedding roundworm eggs at three weeks of age. They can be infected by their mother's milk.

The roundworm, *Ascaris lumbricoides*.

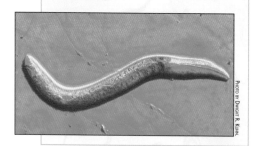

ROUNDWORMS

The roundworms that infect dogs are known scientifically as *Toxocara canis*. They live in the dog's intestines and shed eggs continually. It has been estimated that a dog produces about 6 or more ounces of feces every day. Each ounce of feces averages hundreds of thousands of roundworm eggs. There are no known areas in which dogs roam that do not contain roundworm eggs. The greatest danger of roundworms is that they infect people, too! It is wise to have your dog tested regularly for roundworms.

In young puppies, roundworms cause bloated bellies, diarrhea, coughing and vomiting, and are transmitted from the dam (through blood or milk). Affected puppies will not appear as animated as normal puppies. The worms appear spaghetti-like, measuring as long as 6 inches. Adult dogs can acquire roundworms through coprophagia (eating contaminated feces) or by killing rodents that carry roundworms.

Roundworm infection can kill puppies and cause severe problems in adults, as the hatched larvae travel to the lungs and trachea through the bloodstream. Cleanliness is the best preventative for roundworms. Always pick up after your dog and dispose of feces in appropriate receptacles.

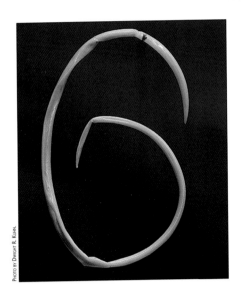

Photo by Dwight R. Kuhn.

HOOKWORMS

In the United States, dog owners have to be concerned about four different species of hookworm, the most common and most serious of which is *Ancylostoma caninum*, which prefers warm climates. The others are *Ancylostoma braziliense*, *Ancylostoma tubaeforme* and *Uncinaria stenocephala*, the latter of which is a concern to dogs living in the Northern US and Canada, as this species prefers cold climates. Hookworms are dangerous to humans as well as to dogs and cats, and can be the cause of severe anemia due to iron deficiency. The worm uses its teeth to attach itself to the dog's intestines and changes the site of its attachment about six times per day. Each time the worm repositions itself, the dog loses blood and can become anemic. *Ancylostoma caninum* is the most likely of the four species to cause anemia in the dog.

Symptoms of hookworm infection include dark stools, weight loss, general weakness, pale coloration and anemia, as well as possible skin problems. Fortunately, hookworms are easily purged from the affected dog with a number of medications that have proven effective. Discuss these with your vet. Most heartworm preventatives include a hookworm insecticide as well.

Owners also must be aware that hookworms can infect humans, who can acquire the larvae through exposure to contaminated feces. Since the worms cannot complete their life cycle on a human, the worms simply infest the skin and cause irritation. This condition is known as cutaneous larva migrans syndrome. As a preventative, use disposable gloves or a "poop-scoop" to pick up your dog's droppings and prevent your dog (or neighborhood cats) from defecating in children's play areas.

The hookworm, *Ancylostoma caninum.*

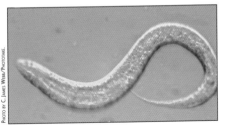

Photo by C. James Webb/Phototake.

The infective stage of the hookworm larva.

TAPEWORMS

Humans, rats, squirrels, foxes, coyotes, wolves and domestic dogs are all susceptible to tapeworm infection. Except in humans, tapeworms are usually not a fatal infection. Infected individuals can harbor 1000 parasitic worms.

Tapeworms, like some other types of worm, are hermaphroditic, meaning male and female in the same worm.

If dogs eat infected rats or mice, or anything else infected with tapeworm, they get the tapeworm disease. One month after attaching to a dog's intestine, the worm starts shedding eggs. These eggs are infective immediately. Infective eggs can live for a few months without a host animal.

The head and rostellum (the round prominence on the scolex) of a tapeworm, which infects dogs and humans.

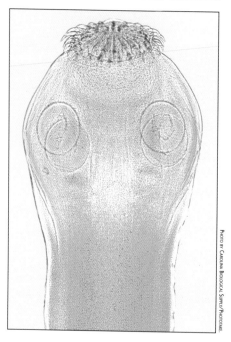

Photo by Carolina Biological Supply/Phototake.

TAPEWORMS

There are many species of tapeworm, all of which are carried by fleas! The most common tapeworm affecting dogs is known as *Dipylidium caninum*. The dog eats the flea and starts the tapeworm cycle. Humans can also be infected with tapeworms—so don't eat fleas! Fleas are so small that your dog could pass them onto your hands, your plate or your food and thus make it possible for you to ingest a flea that is carrying tapeworm eggs.

While tapeworm infection is not life-threatening in dogs (smart parasite!), it can be the cause of a very serious liver disease for humans. About 50% of the humans infected with *Echinococcus multilocularis*, a type of tapeworm that causes alveolar hydatid, perish.

WHIPWORMS

In North America, whipworms are counted among the most common parasitic worms in dogs. The whipworm's scientific name is *Trichuris vulpis*. These worms attach themselves in the lower parts of the intestine, where they feed. Affected dogs may only experience upset tummies, colic and diarrhea. These worms, however, can live for months or years in the dog, beginning their larval stage in the small intestine, spending their adult stage in the large intestine and finally passing infective eggs through the dog's feces. The only way to detect whipworms is through a fecal examination, though this is not always foolproof. Treatment for whipworms is tricky, due to the worms' unusual life-cycle pattern, and very often dogs are reinfected due to exposure to infective eggs on the ground. The whipworm eggs can survive in the environment for as long as five years; thus, cleaning up droppings in your own backyard as well as in public places is absolutely essential for sanitation purposes and the health of your dog and others.

THREADWORMS

Though less common than round-worms, hookworms and those previously mentioned, thread-worms concern dog owners in the Southwestern US and Gulf Coast area where the climate is hot and humid. Living in the small intes-tine of the dog, this worm measures a mere 2 millimeters and is round in shape. Like that of the whipworm, the threadworm's life cycle is very complex and the eggs and larvae are passed through the feces. A deadly disease in humans, *Strongyloides* readily infects people, and the handling of feces is the most common means of trans-mission. Threadworms are most often seen in young puppies; bloody diarrhea and pneumonia are symptoms. Sick puppies must be isolated and treated immedi-ately; vets recommend a follow-up treatment one month later.

HEARTWORM PREVENTATIVES

There are many heartworm preventatives on the market, many of which are sold at your veterinarian's office. These products can be given daily or monthly, depending on the manufacturer's instructions. All of these preventatives contain chemical insecticides directed at killing heartworms, which leads to some controversy among dog owners. In effect, heartworm preventatives are neces-sary evils, though you should determine how necessary based on your pet's lifestyle. There is no doubt that heartworm is a dreadful disease that threatens the lives of dogs. However, the likelihood of your dog's being bitten by an infected mosquito is slim in most places, and a mosquito-repellent (or an herbal remedy such as Wormwood or Black Walnut) is much safer for your dog and will not compromise his immune system (the way heartworm preventatives will). Should you decide to use the tradi-tional preventative "medications," you can consider giving the pill every other or third month. Since the toxins in the pill will kill the heartworms at all stages of develop-ment, the pill would be effective in killing larvae, nymphs or adults, and it takes four months for the larvae to reach the adult stage. Thus, there is no rationale to poison-ing the dog's system on a monthly basis. Lastly, do not give the pill during the winter months since there are no mosquitoes around to pass on their infection, unless you live in a tropical environment.

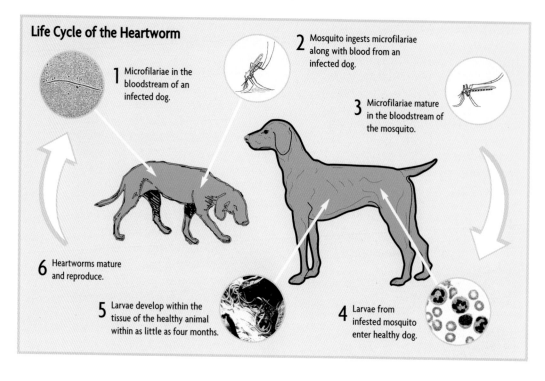

Life Cycle of the Heartworm

1 Microfilariae in the bloodstream of an infected dog.

2 Mosquito ingests microfilariae along with blood from an infected dog.

3 Microfilariae mature in the bloodstream of the mosquito.

6 Heartworms mature and reproduce.

5 Larvae develop within the tissue of the healthy animal within as little as four months.

4 Larvae from infested mosquito enter healthy dog.

HEARTWORMS

Heartworms are thin, extended worms up to 12 inches long, which live in a dog's heart and the major blood vessels surrounding it. Dogs may have up to 200 worms. Symptoms may be loss of energy, loss of appetite, coughing, the development of a pot belly and anemia.

Heartworms are transmitted by mosquitoes. The mosquito drinks the blood of an infected dog and takes in larvae with the blood. The larvae, called microfilariae, develop within the body of the mosquito and are passed on to the next dog bitten after the larvae mature. It takes two to three weeks for the larvae to develop to the infective stage within the body of the mosquito. Dogs are usually treated at about six weeks of age and maintained on a prophylactic dose given monthly.

Blood testing for heartworms is not necessarily indicative of how seriously your dog is infected. Although this is a dangerous disease, it is not easy for a dog to be infected. Discuss the various preventatives with your vet, as there are many different types now available. Together you can decide on a safe course of prevention for your dog.

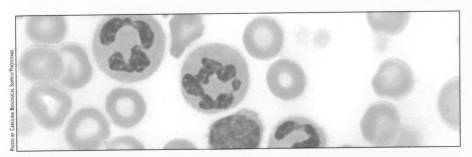

Magnified heart-worm larvae, *Diro-filaria immitis.*

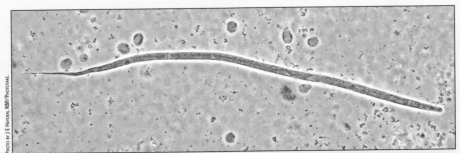

Heartworm, *Diro-filaria immitis.*

The heart of a dog infected with canine heart-worm, *Dirofilaria immitis.*

HOMEOPATHY:
an alternative
to conventional
medicine

"Less is Most"

Using this principle, the strength of a homeopathic remedy is measured by the number of serial dilutions that were undertaken to create it. The greater the number of serial dilutions, the greater the strength of the homeopathic remedy. The potency of a remedy that has been made by making a dilution of 1 part in 100 parts (or 1/100) is 1c or 1cH. If this remedy is subjected to a series of further dilutions, each one being 1/100, a more dilute and stronger remedy is produced. If the remedy is diluted in this way six times, it is called 6c or 6cH. A dilution of 6c is 1 part in 1,000,000,000,000. In general, higher potencies in more frequent doses are better for acute symptoms and lower potencies in more infrequent doses are more useful for chronic, long-standing problems.

CURING OUR DOGS NATURALLY

Holistic medicine means treating the whole animal as a unique, perfect living being. Generally, holistic treatments do not suppress the symptoms that the body naturally produces, as do most medications prescribed by conventional doctors and vets. Holistic methods seek to cure disease by regaining balance and harmony in the patient's environment. Some of these methods include use of nutritional therapy, herbs, flower essences, aromatherapy, acupuncture, massage, chiropractic and, of course, the most popular holistic approach, homeopathy.

Homeopathy is a theory or system of treating illness with small doses of substances which, if administered in larger quantities, would produce the symptoms that the patient already has. This approach is often described as "like cures like." Although modern veterinary medicine is geared toward the "quick fix," homeopathy relies on the belief that, given the time, the body is able to heal itself and return to its natural, healthy state.

Choosing a remedy to cure a problem in our dogs is the difficult part of homeopathy. Consult with your vet for a professional diagnosis of your dog's symptoms. Often these symptoms require immediate conventional care. If your vet is willing and knowledgeable, you may attempt a homeopathic remedy. Be aware that cortisone prevents homeopathic remedies from working. There are hundreds of possibilities and combinations to cure many problems in dogs, from basic physical problems such as excessive shedding, fleas or other parasites, unattractive doggy odor, bad breath, upset tummy, obesity, dry, oily or dull coat, diarrhea, ear problems or eye discharge (including tears and dry or mucousy matter), to behavioral abnormalities such as fear of loud noises, habitual licking, poor appetite, excessive barking and various phobias. From alumina to zincum metallicum, the remedies span the planet and the imagination…from flowers and weeds to chemicals, insect droppings, diesel smoke and volcanic ash.

Using "Like to Treat Like"

Unlike conventional medicines that suppress symptoms, homeopathic remedies treat illnesses with small doses of substances that, if administered in larger quantities, would produce the symptoms that the patient already has. While the same homeopathic remedy can be used to treat different symptoms in different dogs, here are some interesting remedies and their uses.

Apis Mellifica
(made from honey bee venom) can be used for allergies or to reduce swelling that occurs in acutely infected kidneys.

Diesel Smoke
can be used to help control travel sickness.

Calcarea Fluorica
(made from calcium fluoride, which helps harden bone structure) can be useful in treating hard lumps in tissues.

Natrum Muriaticum
(made from common salt, sodium chloride) is useful in treating thin, thirsty dogs.

Nitricum Acidum
(made from nitric acid) is used for symptoms you would expect to see from contact with acids, such as lesions, especially where the skin joins the linings of body orifices or openings such as the lips and nostrils.

Symphytum
(made from the herb Knitbone, *Symphytum officianale*) is used to encourage bones to heal.

Urtica Urens
(made from the common stinging nettle) is used in treating painful, irritating rashes.

The healthy Peke's eyes should be dark and clear, without cloudiness or excessive tearing.

A PET OWNER'S GUIDE TO COMMON OPHTHALMIC DISEASES
by Prof. Dr. Robert L. Peiffer, Jr.

Few would argue that vision is the most important of the cognitive senses, and maintenance of a normal visual system is important for an optimal quality of life. Likewise, pet owners tend to be acutely aware of their pets' eyes and vision, which is important because early detection of ocular disease will optimize therapeutic outcomes. The eye is a sensitive organ with minimal reparative capabilities, and with some diseases, such as glaucoma, uveitis and retinal detachment, early diagnosis and treatment can be critical in terms of whether vision can be preserved. Attention to the eyes is especially important with a breed like the Peke, whose eyes are large and prominent.

Lower entropion, or rolling in of the eyelid, is causing irritation in the left eye of this young dog. Several extra eyelashes, or distichiasis, are present on the lower lid.

The causes of ocular disease are quite varied; the nature of dogs makes their eyes susceptible to traumatic conditions, the most common of which include proptosis of the globe, cat scratch injuries and penetrating wounds from foreign objects, including sticks and air rifle pellets. Infectious diseases caused by bacteria, viruses or fungi may be localized to the eye or part of a systemic infection. Many of the common conditions, including eyelid conformational problems, cataracts, glaucoma and retinal degenerations have genetic bases.

Before acquiring your puppy, it is important to ascertain that both parents have been examined and certified as free of eye disease by a veterinary ophthalmologist. Since many of these genetic diseases can be detected early in life, acquire the pup with the condition that it pass a thorough ophthalmic examination by a qualified specialist.

LID CONFORMATIONAL ABNORMALITIES
Rolling in (entropion) or out (ectropion) of the lids tends to be a breed-related problem. Entropion can involve the upper and/or lower lids. Signs usually appear between 3 and 12 months of age. The irritation caused by the eyelid hairs' rubbing

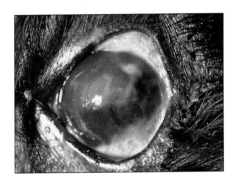

on the surface of the cornea may result in blinking, tearing and damage to the cornea. Ectropion is likewise breed-related and is considered "normal" in hounds, for instance; unlike entropion, which results in acute discomfort, ectropion may cause chronic irritation related to exposure and the pooling of secretions. Most of these cases can be managed medically with daily irrigation with sterile saline and topical antibiotics when required.

EYELASH ABNORMALITIES

Dogs normally have lashes only on the upper lids, in contrast to humans. Occasionally, extra eyelashes may be seen emerging at the eyelid margin (distichiasis) or through the inner surface of the eyelid (ectopic cilia).

CONJUNCTIVITIS

Inflammation of the conjunctiva, the pink tissue that lines the lids and the anterior portion of the sclera, is generally accompanied by redness, discharge and mild discomfort. The majority of cases are associated with either bacterial infections or dry-eye syndrome. Fortunately, topical medications are generally effective in curing or controlling the problem.

DRY-EYE SYNDROME

Dry-eye syndrome (keratoconjunctivitis sicca) is a common cause of external ocular disease. Discharge is typically thick and sticky, and keratitis is a frequent component; any breed can be affected. While some cases can be associated with toxic effects of drugs, including the sulfa antibiotics, the cause in the majority of the cases cannot be determined and is assumed to be immune-mediated.

Keratoconjunctivitis sicca, seen here in the right eye of a middle-aged dog, causes a characteristic thick mucous discharge as well as secondary corneal changes.

Left: Prolapse of the gland of the third eyelid in the right eye of a pup. Right: In this case, in the right eye of a young dog, the prolapsed gland can be seen emerging between the edge of the third eyelid and the corneal surface.

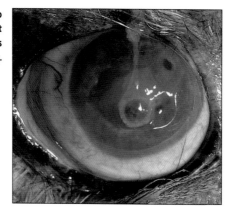

Multiple deep ulcerations affect the cornea of this middle-aged dog.

PROLAPSE OF THE GLAND OF THE THIRD EYELID

In this condition, commonly referred to as *cherry eye*, the gland of the third eyelid, which produces about one-third of the aqueous phase of the tear film and is normally situated within the anterior orbit, prolapses to emerge as a pink fleshy mass protruding over the edge of the third eyelid, between the third eyelid and the cornea. The condition usually develops during the first year of life and, while mild irritation may result, the condition is unsightly as much as anything else.

CORNEAL DISEASE

The cornea is the clear front part of the eye that provides the first step in the collection of light on its journey to be eventually focused onto the retina, and most corneal diseases will be manifested by alterations in corneal transparency. The cornea is an exquisitely innervated tissue, and

Lipid deposition can occur as a primary inherited dystrophy, or secondarily to hypercholesterolemia (in dogs frequently associated with hypothyroidism), chronic corneal inflammation or neoplasia. The deposits in this dog's eye assume an oval pattern in the center of the cornea.

defects in corneal integrity are accompanied by pain, which is demonstrated by squinting.

Corneal ulcers, one of the most common problems in the Peke, may occur secondarily to trauma or to irritation from entropion or ectopic cilia. In middle-aged or older dogs, epithelial ulcerations may occur spontaneously due to an inherent defect; these are referred to as indolent or Boxer ulcers, in recognition of the breed in which we see the condition most frequently. Infection may occur secondarily. Ulcers can be potentially blinding conditions; severity is dependent upon the size and depth of the ulcer and other complicating features.

Non-ulcerative keratitis tends to have an immune-mediated component and is managed by topical immunosuppressants, usually corticosteroids. Corneal edema can occur in elderly dogs. It is due to a failure of the corneal endothelial "pump."

The cornea responds to chronic irritation by transforming into skin-like tissue that is

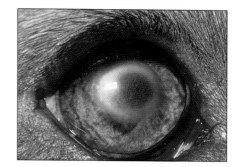

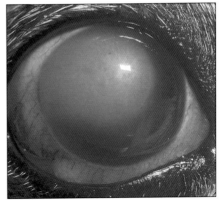

evident clinically by pigmentation, scarring and vascularization; some cases may respond to tear stimulants, lubricants and topical corticosteroids, while others benefit from surgical narrowing of the eyelid opening in order to enhance corneal protection.

UVEITIS

Inflammation of the vascular tissue of the eye–the uvea—is a common and potentially serious disease in dogs. While it may occur secondarily to trauma or other intraocular diseases, such as cataracts, most commonly uveitis is associated

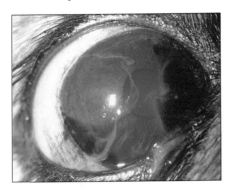

with some type of systemic infectious or neoplastic process. Uncontrolled, uveitis can lead to blinding cataracts, glaucoma and/or retinal detachments, and aggressive symptomatic therapy with dilating agents (to prevent pupillary adhesions) and anti-inflammatories are critical.

GLAUCOMA

The eye is essentially a hollow fluid-filled sphere, and the pressure within is maintained by regulation of the rate of fluid production and fluid egress at 10–20 mms of mercury. The retinal cells are extremely sensitive to elevations of intraocular pressure and, unless controlled, permanent blindness can occur within hours to days. In acute glaucoma, the conjunctiva becomes congested, the cornea cloudy, the pupil moderate and fixed; the eye is generally painful and avisual. Increased constant signs of discomfort will accompany chronic cases.

Corneal edema can develop as a slowly progressive process in elderly Boston Terriers, Miniature Dachshunds and Miniature Poodles, as well as others, as a result of the inability of the corneal endothelial "pump" to maintain a state of dehydration.

Medial pigmentary keratitis in this dog is associated with irritation from prominent facial folds.

Glaucoma in the dog most commonly occurs as a sudden extreme elevation of intraocular pressure, frequently to three to four times the norm. The eye of this dog demonstrates the common signs of episcleral injection, or redness; mild diffuse corneal cloudiness, due to edema; and a mid-sized fixed pupil.

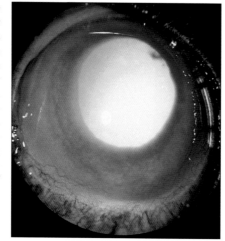

Management of glaucoma is one of the most challenging situations that the veterinary ophthalmologist faces; in spite of intense efforts, many of these cases will result in blindness.

CATARACTS AND LENS DISLOCATION

Cataracts are the most common blinding condition in dogs; fortunately, they are readily amenable to surgical intervention, with excellent results in terms of restoration of vision and replace-

ment of the cataractous lens with a synthetic one. Most cataracts in dogs are inherited; less commonly cataracts can be secondary to trauma; other ocular diseases, including uveitis, glaucoma, lens luxation and retinal degeneration; or secondary to an underlying systemic metabolic disease, including diabetes and Cushing's disease. Signs include a progressive loss of the bright dark appearance of the pupil, which is replaced by a blue-gray hazy appearance. In this respect, cataracts need to be distinguished from the normal aging process of nuclear sclerosis, which occurs in middle-aged or older animals, and has minimal effect on vision.

Lens dislocation occurs in dogs and frequently leads to secondary glaucoma; early removal of the dislocated lens is generally curative.

RETINAL DISEASE

Retinal degenerations are usually inherited, but may be associated with vitamin E deficiency in dogs.

Left: The typical posterior subcapsular cataract appears between one and two years of age, but rarely progresses to where the animal has visual problems. Right: Inherited cataracts generally appear between three and six years of age, and progress to the stage seen where functional vision is significantly impaired.

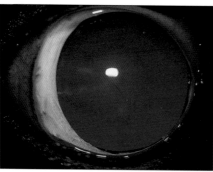

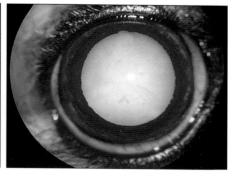

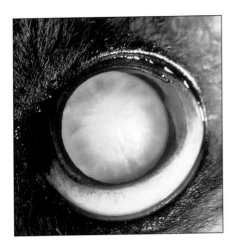

While signs are variable, most frequently one notes a decrease in vision over a period of months, which typically starts out as night blindness. The cause of a more rapid loss of vision due to retinal degeneration occurs over days to weeks and is labeled *sudden acquired retinal degeneration* or SARD; the outcome, however, is unfortunately usually similar to inherited and nutritional condi-

tions, as the retinal tissues possess minimal regenerative capabilities. Most pets, however, with a bit of extra care and attention, show an amazing ability to adapt to an avisual world, and can be maintained as pets with a satisfactory quality of life.

Detachment of the retina—due to accumulation of blood between the retina and the underling uvea, which is called the *choroid*—can occur secondarily to retinal tears or holes, or tractional forces within the eye, or as a result of uveitis. These types of detachments may be amenable to surgical repair if diagnosed early.

OPTIC NERVE

Optic neuritis, or inflammation of the nerve that connects the eye with the brain stem, is a relatively uncommon condition that presents usually with rather sudden loss of vision and widely dilated non-responsive pupils.

Anterior lens luxation can occur as a primary disease in the terrier breeds, or secondarily to trauma. The fibers that hold the lens in place rupture and the lens may migrate through the pupil to be situated in front of the iris. Secondary glaucoma is a frequent and significant complication that can be avoided if the dislocated lens is removed surgically.

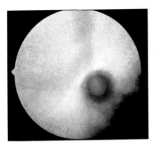 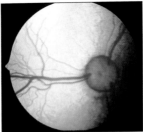 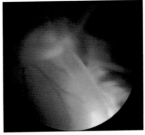 

Left: The posterior pole of a normal fundus is shown; prominent are the head of the optic nerve and the retinal blood vessels. The retina is transparent, and the prominent green tapetum is seen superiorly. Center: An eye with inherited retinal dysplasia is depicted. The tapetal retina superior to the optic disc is disorganized, with multifocal areas of hyperplasia of the retinal pigment epithelium. Right: Severe collie eye anomaly and a retinal detachment; this eye is unfortunately blind.

When you purchase your Pekingese, you will make it clear to the breeder whether you want one just as a loveable companion and pet, or if you hope to be buying a Peke with show prospects. No reputable breeder will sell you a young puppy and tell you that it is *definitely* of show quality, for so much can go wrong during the early months of a puppy's development. If you plan to show, what you will hopefully have acquired is a puppy with "show potential."

To the novice, exhibiting a Pekingese in the show ring may look easy, but it takes a lot of hard work and devotion to do top winning at a show such as the prestigious Westminster Kennel Club dog show, not to mention a little luck, too!

The first concept that the canine novice learns when watching a dog show is that each dog first competes against members of his own breed. Once the judge has selected the best member of each breed (Best of Breed), provided that the show is judged on a Group system, that chosen dog will compete with other dogs in his group. Finally, the dogs chosen first in each group will compete for Best in Show.

The second concept that you must understand is that the dogs are not actually compared against one another. The judge compares each dog against the breed's standard, the written description of the ideal specimen that is approved by the American Kennel Club (AKC). While some early breed standards were indeed based on specific dogs that were famous or popular, many dedicated enthusiasts say that a perfect specimen, as described in the standard, has never walked into a show ring, has never been bred and, to the woe of dog breeders around the globe, does not exist. Breeders attempt to get as close to this ideal as possible with every litter, but theoretically the "perfect" dog is so elusive that it is impossible. (And if the "perfect" dog were born, breeders and judges would never agree that it was indeed "perfect.")

If you are interested in exploring the world of dog showing, your best bet is to join your local breed club or the national parent club, which is the Pekingese Club of America. These clubs often host both regional and national specialties, shows only for Pekingese, which can include conformation as well as obedience and agility trials. Even if you have no intention of competing with your Peke, a specialty is a like a festival for lovers of the breed who congregate to share their favorite topic: the Pekingese! Clubs also send out newsletters, and some organize training days and seminars in order that people may learn more about their chosen breed. To locate the breed club closest to you, contact the American Kennel Club, which furnishes the rules and regulations for all of these events plus general dog registration and other basic requirements of dog ownership.

In the US, the American Kennel Club offers three kinds of conformation shows: an all-breed show (for all AKC-recognized breeds), a specialty show (for one breed only, usually sponsored by the parent club) and a Group show (for all breeds in the group).

For a dog to become an AKC champion of record, the dog must accumulate 15 points at the shows from at least three different judges, including two "majors." A "major" is defined as a three-, four- or five-point win, and the number of points per win is determined by the number of dogs entered in the show on that day. Depending on the breed, the number of points that are awarded varies. In more popular breeds, more dogs are needed to rack up the points; in less popular breeds, fewer dogs are needed. The Pekingese is a popular show dog that usually attracts large entries at shows.

At any dog show, only one dog and one bitch of each breed can win points. Dog showing does not offer "co-ed" classes. Dogs and bitches never compete against each other in the classes. Non-champion dogs are called "class dogs" because they compete in one of five

Training, grooming and handling a show Pekingese are challenging, but the rewards can be wonderful. One of these worthy participants will soon be deemed the winner by the judge.

CLUB CONTACTS

You can get information about dog shows from the national kennel clubs:

American Kennel Club
5580 Centerview Dr., Raleigh, NC 27606-3390
www.akc.org

United Kennel Club
100 E. Kilgore Road, Kalamazoo, MI 49002
www.ukcdogs.com

Canadian Kennel Club
89 Skyway Ave., Suite 100, Etobicoke, Ontario
   M9W 6R4, Canada
    www.ckc.ca

   The Kennel Club
   1-5 Clarges St., Piccadilly, London
   W1Y 8AB, UK
  www.the-kennel-club.org.uk

classes. Dogs are entered in a particular class depending on age and previous show wins. To begin, there is the Puppy Class (for 6- to 9-month-olds and for 9- to 12-month-olds); this class is followed by the Novice Class (for dogs that have not won any first prizes except in the Puppy Class or three first prizes in the Novice Class and have not accumulated any points toward their champion title); the Bred-by-Exhibitor Class (for dogs handled by their breeders or by one of the breeder's immediate family); the American-bred Class (for dogs bred in the US); and the Open Class (for any dog that is not a champion).

The judge at the show begins judging the Puppy Class, first dogs and then bitches, and proceeds through the classes. The judge places his winners first through fourth in each class. In the Winners Class, the first-place winners of each class compete with one another to determine Winners Dog and Winners Bitch. The judge also places a Reserve Winners Dog and Reserve Winners Bitch, which could be awarded the points in the case of a disqualification. The Winners Dog and Winners Bitch are the two that are awarded the points for the breed; they then compete with any champions of record entered in the show. The judge reviews the Winners Dog, Winners Bitch and all of the champions to select his Best of Breed. The Best of Winners is selected between the Winners Dog and Winners Bitch. Were one of these two to be selected Best of Breed, he or she would automatically be named Best of Winners as well. Finally the judge selects his Best of Opposite Sex to the Best of Breed winner.

At a Group show or all-breed show, the Best of Breed winners from each breed then compete against one another for Group One through Group Four. The judge compares each Best of Breed to his respective breed standard, and the dog that most closely lives up to the ideal for his breed is selected as Group One. Finally, all seven group winners (from the Toy Group,

Sporting Group, Hound Group, etc.) compete for Best in Show.

To find out about dog shows in your area, you can subscribe to the American Kennel Club's monthly magazine, the *American Kennel Gazette*, and the accompanying *Events Calendar*. You can also look in your local newspaper for advertisements for dog shows in your area or go on the Internet to the AKC's website, http:www.akc.org.

If your Pekingese is six months of age or older and registered with the AKC, you can enter him a dog show where the breed is offered classes. Provided that your Peke does not have a disqualifying fault, he can compete. Only unaltered dogs can be entered in a dog show, so if you have spayed or neutered your Pekingese, you cannot compete in conformation shows. The reason for this is simple. Dog shows are the main forum to prove which representatives of a breed are worthy of being bred. Only dogs that have achieved championships—the AKC "seal of approval" for quality in pure-bred dogs—should be bred. Altered dogs, however, can participate in other AKC events such as obedience trials and the Canine Good Citizen program.

Before you actually step into the ring, you would be well advised to sit back and observe the judge's ring procedure. If it is your first time in the ring, do not be over-anxious and run to the front of the line. It is much better to stand back and study how the exhibitor in front of you is performing. The judge asks each handler to "stack" the dog, hopefully showing the dog off to his best advantage. The judge will observe the dog from a distance and from different angles, and approach the dog to check his teeth, overall structure, alertness and muscle tone, as well as consider how well the dog "conforms" to the standard. Most importantly, the judge will have the exhibitor move the dog around the ring in some pattern that he should specify (another advantage to not going first, but always listen since some judges change their directions—and the judge is always right!). Finally, the judge will give the dog one last look before moving on to the next exhibitor.

Even juniors can get involved in the dog show scene, and the Peke is an ideal dog to have on the end of a junior's leash.

If you are not in the top four in your class at your first show, do not be discouraged. Be patient and consistent, and you may eventually find yourself in a winning line-up. Remember that the winners were once in your shoes and have devoted many hours and much money to earn the placement. If you find that your dog is losing every time and never getting a nod, it may be time to consider a different dog sport or to just enjoy your Peke as a pet. Parent clubs offer other events, such as agility, obedience and more, which may be of interest to the owner of a well-trained Pekingese.

OBEDIENCE TRIALS
Obedience trials in the US trace back to the early 1930s, when organized obedience training was developed to demonstrate how well dog and owner could work together. The pioneer of obedience trials is Mrs. Helen Whitehouse Walker, a Standard Poodle fancier, who designed a series of exercises after the Associated Sheep, Police Army Dog Society of Great Britain. Since the days of Mrs. Walker, obedience trials have grown by leaps and bounds, and today there are over 2,000 trials held in the US every year, with more than 100,000 dogs competing. Any registered AKC dog can enter an obedience trial, regardless of conformational disqualifications or neutering.

Obedience trials are divided into three levels of progressive difficulty. At the first level, the Novice, dogs compete for the title Companion Dog (CD); at the intermediate level, the Open, dogs compete for the title Companion Dog Excellent (CDX); and at the advanced level, the Utility, dogs compete for the title Utility Dog (UD). Classes are sub-divided into "A" (for beginners) and "B" (for more experienced handlers). A perfect score at any level is 200, and a dog must score 170 or better to earn a "leg," of which three are needed to earn the title. To earn points, the dog must score more than 50% of the available points in each exercise; the possible points range from 20 to 40.

Each level consists of a different set of exercises. In the Novice level, the dog must heel on- and off-leash, come, long sit, long down and stand for examination. These skills are the basic ones required for a well-behaved "Companion Dog." The Open level requires that the dog perform the same exercises as above but without a leash for extended lengths of time, as well as retrieve a dumbbell, broad jump and drop on recall. In the Utility level, dogs must perform ten difficult exercises, including scent discrimination, hand signals for basic commands, directed jump and directed retrieve.

Once a dog has earned the UD title, he can compete with other proven obedience dogs for the

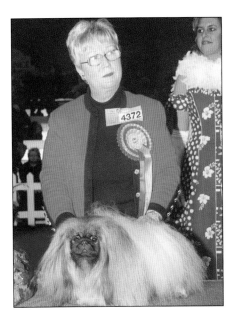

Winning the Toy Group at an FCI show in Amsterdam, this Pekingese has proven his owner proud.

coveted title of Utility Dog Excellent (UDX), which requires that the dog win "legs" in ten shows. Utility Dogs who earn "legs" in Open B and Utility B earn points toward their Obedience Trial Champion title. In 1977, the title Obedience Trial Champion (OTCh.) was established by the AKC. To become an OTCh., a dog needs to earn 100 points, which requires three first places in Open B and Utility under three different judges.

The Grand Prix of obedience trials, the AKC National Obedience Invitational gives qualifying Utility Dogs the chance to win the newest and highest title: National Obedience Champion (NOC). Only the top 25 ranked obedience dogs, plus any dog ranked in the top 3 in his breed, are allowed to compete.

AGILITY TRIALS

Having had its origins in the UK back in 1977, AKC agility had its official beginning in the US in August 1994, when the first licensed agility trials were held. The AKC allows all registered breeds (including Miscellaneous Class breeds) to participate, providing the dog is 12 months of age or older. Agility is designed so that the handler demonstrates how well the dog can work at his side. The handler directs his dog over an obstacle course that includes jumps as well as tires, the dog walk, weave poles, pipe tunnels, collapsed tunnels, etc. While working his way through the course, the dog must keep one eye and ear on the handler and the rest of his body on the course. The handler gives verbal and hand signals to guide the dog through the course.

The first organization to promote agility trials in the US was the United States Dog Agility Association, Inc. (USDAA), which was established in 1986 and spawned numerous member clubs around the country. Both the USDAA and the AKC offer titles to winning dogs.

Agility is great fun for dog and owner with many rewards for everyone involved. Interested owners should join a training club that has obstacles and experienced agility handlers who can introduce you and your dog to the "ropes" (and tires, tunnels, etc.).

INDEX

My Pekingese

PUT YOUR PUPPY'S FIRST PICTURE HERE

Dog's Name _____

Date _____ Photographer _____